# Out of the Dark

# Out of the Dark

## *Into the* Garden of Hope

Sam Keo, PsyD

iUniverse, Inc.
Bloomington

# OUT OF THE DARK
## INTO THE GARDEN OF HOPE

iUniverse books may be ordered through booksellers or by contacting:

iUniverse
1663 Liberty Drive
Bloomington, IN 47403
www.iuniverse.com
1-800-Authors (1-800-288-4677)

ISBN: 978-1-4620-6648-3 (sc)
ISBN: 978-1-4620-6647-6 (hc)
ISBN: 978-1-4620-6646-9 (ebk)

Library of Congress Control Number: 2011962176

Printed in the United States of America

iUniverse rev. date: 12/16/2011

# ─── CONTENTS ───

To my wife, Bonavy, the love of my life,
who has been alongside me through the difficult times. She is
my motivator, my encourager, my technical supporter, and my
cheerleader.
Bonavy, you are my forever life partner!

To my three sons,
Douglas, Beauregard, and Nickolas,
who make me always want to be a better dad and who
give me reason to live.

In loving memory of my parents,
father, Keo Kim, and mother, He Savoan,
who inspired me to seek higher education.
May you rest in peace.

In loving memory of my four little brothers,
Pich, Duke, Arun, and Aren, and my sister, Savaing, whose lives
were taken away prematurely by the cruel regime of Pol Pot and his
puppets.

In loving memory of my grandma, my aunt, my uncle,
my two brothers-in-law, my nieces and nephews, and the 1.7
million Cambodians who perished under the Pol Pot regime. May
they rest in peace.

# ACKNOWLEDGMENTS

I would not have been able to complete this emotional and overwhelming book without the support of many of my coworkers; friends; and, most of all, my family. They are my faithful supporters, cheerleaders, and believers. I want to thank them all for motivating, encouraging, and challenging me and for touching my life in so many ways. I want to thank my loving family, who gave me support no matter what.

There are people and groups who are very special to me, and I feel that I must recognize them in this acknowledgment. These individuals are as follows:

To our good friends for nearly twenty years, Bill and Kathleen Murray: You have been there for me, my wife, my children, my brother, and my sister whenever we needed your help. When I was struggling and suffering with PTSD, Bill, you took me out of the situation and allowed me to work on my issues while I was under your supervision in the county. Several years ago, when my brother was hospitalized in Cambodia and we were experiencing financial hardship, Bill and Kathleen, both of you were kind and gracious enough to help him with my brother's hospital bills, even though you had never met him before. When my book was completed, I asked you, Bill, to read it and give me your feedback, and you agreed without hesitation. These are only a very few examples of your and Kathleen's kindness that has touched me and my family.

To Mark S. Painter, Jeff of New York, and Jeff of Philadelphia: You all helped me to get to know America during my first year in the United States. You told me about the endless opportunities that I could obtain here. I learned more from you about America and its people than you will ever know. You are the first three people who injected into me so many positive views of America. I am truly glad that you were the first Americans I had the pleasure of getting to know.

To Ms. Kim Sasaki, my first manager in Los Angeles County: You are kind and understanding. When I was in my emotional turmoil, you gave me time to vent and release my frustration. You also contributed to my brother's hospital bill in Cambodia, and you do not even know him. I am touched.

I also want to thank Bing Lau, a friend at LAC-DMH who introduced me to Ms. Beverly Gray, the author of *Ron Howard: From Mayberry to the Moon . . . . and Beyond*. Ms. Gray gave me an idea about how to convert my short essay into this book. I am thankful to both Ms. Gray and Ms. Lau.

To my training division colleagues at the County of Los Angeles, Department of Mental Health: You are not just colleagues; you are my friends. It was so hard for me to leave you after our seven years together. You guys are like my family to me. I am glad that we still keep in touch and grateful for your presence in my life.

To *all* my friends at the Orange County Behavioral Health Services, where I spent my first fifteen years as a health-care employee: Thank you for giving me the opportunity to begin my professional career in mental health with you. I was groomed to be who I am today in the mental health profession because of all of you. You are too many to mention by name, but you know who you are!

Finally, to Bonavy, Douglas, Beauregard, and Nickolas: You are the bliss and blessing of my life, and all of you are the keys to my success. You inspired me and stood by me as I completed this book. You have been the recipients of many of my mistakes and failures. Thank you for your patience and tolerance. You are my heroes. You give meaning to my existence. You are everything to me, and you are my loves.

# AUTHOR'S NOTE

This book is the product of a short essay I did and presented in one of my doctoral classes in 1994. I moved myself and my classmates emotionally during the presentation. After my speech, many of my classmates encouraged me to extend the essay into a book.

I began to write this book in the summer of 1994. Whenever I got to the traumatic scenes, I found myself thrown back into the experiences, as if they were happening all over again. I was stressed and traumatized by the experiences. I took a couple months off from writing, and then a couple of years, before I had the courage to come back to write again. That is why *Out of the Dark* took me seventeen years to complete.

The people, places, and events described in this book are based on my recollection to the best of my memory's ability.

# COMMENTS FROM FRIENDS:

"This book is a captivating account of personal struggle for life in the midst of Cambodia's struggle for identity and the courageous choice of life over the fatal scares of war. The author's perseverance and purpose is human dignity reborn."
*Bill Murray, MA, County of Orange, Behavioral Health Care Administrator*

"I have known Dr. Keo for over 10 years. He shares his own personal experiences as a trauma survivor and his story will undoubtedly inspire those who share similar traumatic experiences. This is a courageous account of his daily struggles which will enlighten readers while also instilling hope that it is possible to recover and thrive after experiencing adversities."
*Youngsook Kim-Sasaki, RN, MSN, Mental Health Services Administrator*

"Dr. Keo has provided us with an amazing story of a harrowing experience and life-long journey to overcome the scars of man's inhumanity. His dedication to working in mental health and within the Asian-American community, are the testaments to the resiliency of the human spirit and to the notion of altruism."
*Ira Lesser, MD, Harbor-UCLA Medical Center, Chair, Department of Psychiatry*

"When Sam gave his acceptance speech, I was very impressed and touched by his story. I had no knowledge of the losses he suffered and I gained even more respect due to his ability to overcome and achieve so much despite insurmountable obstacles. His story reflects his personal journey, but also those of Cambodians in general. He represents the best in not only the Cambodian people but all of us."
*Mitsuru Kubota, PhD, DMH Mental Health Clinical Program Head*

"Sam is an extraordinaire individual who has transcended personal strife and tragedy to become a source of inspiration to so many people he has touched through his personal and professional life. Capturing his story in a biographical literary work is not only a worthy tribute to a special individual but also an important means to reach a greater audience that will surely glean inspiration and hope from his compelling tale of the human spirit's ability to triumph over incredible odds. This book is sure to resonate with a wide audience on many levels and should serve as the source for a theatrical adaptation which would be a logical evolution in disseminating Sam's amazing story."
*Luis E. Escalante, MSW, MPA*

"This story was very powerful. It made me realize how much I took for granted."
*Janice Michelle Friend, LCSW, LAC-DMH Training Division*

"This book will inspire readers to keep their hope and dream alive. I am very proud of Sam's accomplishment. He is not only represented himself, he truly represents all of us, Cambodians, as a community in USA. His endurance and hardship have paid off. Good Job, brother!"
*Sovicheth El, Long Beach Asian Pacific Mental Health Center*

"With personal trauma behind him, and a new hope before him, Sam came to America. In this book, he relates to us his own story of struggles and persistence even though told by his Cambodian case worker that he would not amount to anything but a slave to an American. He refused to accept that, and applied himself to all the challenging opportunities before him; and with sheer determination, he overcame all the difficulties and became a success. Sam has realized his dream of becoming an effective psychologist to help others who are facing traumatic experiences."
*Freda Cheung, PhD, Harbor-UCLA Medical Center, Biomedical Research Institute*

"It is, indeed, a blessing for us to read about Sam's personal experiences of trauma in Cambodia. With our busy lives and preoccupation with demands of everyday living in the Unites States, stories of the killing fields seem to be so far away. It has been too easy for us to neglect experiences of horror in many other parts of the world or even in a different part of our

neighborhood.  It has been too easy to forget the incredible harm that we are all capable of doing to our fellow human beings.  It has been too easy to lose our focus on the human potential to survive great tragedies and message of hope and humanity.  I feel truly humble and grateful for Sam's personal stories as well as the messages behind these moving stories."
*Timothy Chiang, PhD, Coastal Asian Pacific Mental Health and Family Center*

"This book is about a personal journey of a man who experienced harsh and cruel periods in life.  The story of this man touches you in many ways, such as, his story teaches you that life is precious, and that it is to your own benefit to continue to persevere through tumultuous circumstances that you encounter in life, because it is through perseverance and patience that you build a character, purpose and meaning in life.   Dr. Keo is a special man because he overcame his life struggles and became a contributing citizen, not only, by his words, but also, by his actions, accomplishments, and deeds."
*Gregory Tchakmakjian, PhD, SA3 Program Administrator*

"Sam, you continually make your old professor proud."
*Casey Dorman, PhD, Alliant International University*

# ──FOREWORD──

This is an invaluable eyewitness account of what one man endured on the killing fields of Cambodia. Sam Keo describes in startlingly graphic detail how he survived when so many others met senseless deaths and how his suffering at the hands of the Khmer Rouge took its toll on him many years later. Sam's memoir shows what human beings are capable of, for better and for worse.

Beverly Gray
Santa Monica, California
Author, *Roger Corman: Blood-Sucking Vampire, Flesh-Eating Cockroaches, and Driller Killers* and *Ron Howard: From Mayberry to the Moon . . . and Beyond*

# —CHAPTER 1—

# Cambodia in a Nutshell

As human beings, we are constantly evolving to adapt to environmental and political changes. We have survived natural disasters; man-made disasters; and of course, many wars. As we encounter these constant changes, we learn to adapt. Darwin stated that species would become extinct if they failed to adapt to change. Changes can be desirable or undesirable, fruitful or wasteful. Changes can also be considered major or minor.

I have lived through many major changes throughout my life. I had eleven brothers and sisters. Only six of us survived the holocaust of change that engulfed our motherland, Cambodia. In the following account, I will tell how I was able to survive the holocaust and its residual effects.

\*   \*   \*

The country of Cambodia is about the size of Missouri. It gained its independence from France on November 9, 1953, through the Geneva Convention (after nearly ninety years of colonialism). King Sihanouk abdicated the throne to his father in order to be elected prime minister. He became the head of state after his father's death in 1960. He ruled Cambodia from 1955 until the collapse of the monarchy in March 1970, when General Lon Nol and Prince Sisowath Sirik Matak overthrew the Royalist government with the help of the Republican Party. This effort was backed by the United States government. Cambodia was governed by a democratic government, the Cambodian Republican Party, from 1970 to 1975. In April 1975, the Khmer Communists, also known as the Khmer Rouge, backed by China and Communist Vietnam, overcame the republic. The

Khmer Rouge committed atrocities, including the genocide of its own people, and turned its back on Communist Vietnam.

In January 1979, the People's Republic of Kampuchea, backed by the Vietnamese and the Soviet Union, drove the Khmer Rouge out of power. A new government was installed and monitored by the Vietnamese government. Khmer Rouge, Khmer Royalist, and Khmer Buddhism factions formed guerrilla militias to fight back. In October 1991, all four factions signed a treaty in Paris, agreeing to a cease-fire. The agreement allowed United Nations forces to monitor a fair election in May 1993. It was the most expensive election ever sponsored in United Nations history.

The Khmer Rouge violated the treaty just before the election was to be held. The United Nations threatened to eject the organization from participating in the election process. As a result, the Khmer Rouge withdrew, and they continued their fight.

In the election, the Royalists won most seats in the parliament. The three parties voted for the country to be ruled as a monarchy with two prime ministers. The government crowned Prince Sihanouk king. The major political parties had difficulty getting along, and at some point, their inability to do so resulted in bloodshed. The Khmer Rouge continued the war against the government, and innocent people continued to lose their lives. All of these movements tremendously impacted the lives of my family and the Cambodian people.

The people of Cambodia lived under the monarchy, with Prince Sihanouk as the head of state, until March 1970. The illiteracy rate in Cambodia was high prior to that, and the country's main economic resource was agriculture. Since most peasants were uneducated, it was easy for the prince to gain and maintain his dictatorship. His government viewed freedom and liberty as the creators of anarchy. Whoever advocated freedom of speech or freedom of the press before 1970 was either prosecuted as a traitor (*kbat cheat*) or simply disappeared. Prince Sihanouk allowed his government to capture any suspect. Government executioners paraded each alleged traitor around before placing him or her in front of the firing squad to be shot publicly. Both the parades and the executions were filmed, and the final shot was a close-up of the deceased's head. These films were shown in movie theatres as previews before the featured presentation and at all the temples' religious celebrations for which the temple committees rented movies to show to the public. This deterrent tactic worked nicely on us common people.

The prince's government and supporters even created songs to praise him and to curse his enemies. As children, we were taught these songs, and we sang them innocently.

However, Prince Sihanouk was credited with promoting education during the 1950s and '60s. He mandated that every Cambodian adult must be able to read Khmer. Police randomly put up barricades in the streets to give people a reading exam. Those who were not able to read would face a heavy fine. This requirement forced many Cambodians to attend night school to learn to read. Peasants who were too old to learn or had learning difficulties had to avoid authorities for fear of being fined. My mother, who was illiterate, had to leave five young children at home to attend night school. Thankfully, she was able to learn, and she credited her reading ability to the strict requirement of the government.

In addition to mandating that everyone must be able to read, Prince Sihanouk provided scholarships to intellectuals to study abroad. Unfortunately for him, many of them turned against him after they had received their education. They detested the ideology that guided his governing of the country. This often antimonarchist educated class shared its view of true democracy with fellow Cambodians. Leftists believed that Prince Sihanouk was using his prestige to take advantage of the peasants. Those who did not agree with his governing style and who loved the freedoms of press and speech fled the country and lived abroad for survival.

The prince's government viewed the United States as an evil empire, and the authorities made us believe this view was accurate. His government, with his approval, rejected economic aid from the United States in 1963. They cooperated directly with the Communists of Vietnam, who needed Cambodian territory for bases and supply lines. They used the police and military to suppress those who challenged the prince's authority.

In 1970, while Prince Sihanouk was in Paris, General Lon Nol assumed control of the government. Prince Sihanouk's half brother, Prince Sisowath Sirik Matak, and several high-ranking officers who had close connections with the United States government assisted this coup d'état. Western governments quickly supported the new government. General Lon Nol introduced a genuine democracy to his people. He empowered them with freedom of speech, press, and expression. Cambodia had been living under a suppressed regime for centuries before these events. When twentieth-century ways of life were introduced to the Cambodian people, they quickly exercised and embraced them as God-given rights. Soon, in my opinion, they started to abuse their rights, and the country was in turmoil. General Lon Nol's regime appeared unstable, with many riots and increased corruption. People lost faith in the government.

In an attempt to restore his power, Prince Sihanouk asked North Vietnam and the Vietcong for help. He joined the Khmer Rouge to form a fighting force. The guerrilla forces appeared to be much stronger than the government forces, physically and psychologically. They quickly gained trust from the people, especially the uneducated, rural communities. They won the battle on April 17, 1975.

What followed was four years of terror for the Cambodian people—a holocaust that would leave many of those who survived with wounds that would never heal.

# CHAPTER 2

# Leaving Cambodia

My heart was pounding as I walked toward the Thai Airways terminal in Poh Chintong International Airport, Cambodia. I was about to leave my family for the second time. My thoughts were racing. I wanted to give my family members big hugs, but our family culture stopped me from hugging them. I was afraid that I may offend them. I dragged my feet off the ground to climb up the stairs toward the plane. My wife, who was in the traditional Cambodian blouse with a necklace made of jasmine flowers, appeared very sad. Her facial expression was empty, void of her usual smile. I wished I could see my own expression. I was sure that my wife's sadness must be the result of the pain and anguish I was feeling. She held my hand and pulled me up. I waved good-bye to my sisters and brothers.

"Good-bye, sisters; good-bye brothers; good-bye nieces and nephews. I am going to miss you all very much," I said to them in Cambodian.

"We will miss you too. Please come back soon; at least come to see us once a year," my sister responded.

I waved good-bye to my in-laws, my nieces, and my nephews, who I had just met for the first time during the past three weeks. I slowly walked to my assigned seat and sat down. As I pressed my face against my porthole window, I saw my family lined up behind the barbwire fence. Some of them climbed on the fence; others sat on the poles of the fence waving. My face against the glass window, I whispered to them, "I will never forget you. I will miss you so much. I promise to come back and do whatever I can to make your life a little bit better."

The engine roared, and the plane started to move slowly toward the runway. A couple of my brothers and nephews ran along the fence to keep pace with the plane. I looked at them; my pulse was racing, my chest was tight, and my heart was pounding, beating faster and faster. Tears began to pour down my cheeks. I let my thoughts run.

It was early August 1992. The soil was supposed to be wet and ready for the plowing season. But instead, there was only brown grass due to a drought. Cambodia's main economic resource had always been agriculture. If the farmers couldn't plant rice, how would they survive?

As soon as the plane took off, I broke out in sobs, crying loudly. I couldn't stop my tears. Oh God, I lost control of myself. My wife tried to comfort me. I didn't care if people saw me cry. I just didn't care. If they were friends, they would understand. If they weren't, it did not matter what they thought of me. As the plane stabilized in the air, the flight attendant came to offer help. I continued to cry. I felt no shame for crying. I knew my family on the ground probably cried much harder.

Why did this separation seem like a traumatic event? Prior to this visit, the last time I had seen my family was September 1979. My brothers and sisters were still single, and my mother was still alive.

My mother had suggested that I should go visit my brother, Samith, in Pursat Province, 186 kilometers from Phnom Penh. She said that I might find a government job there. Heeding her advice I left, taking my youngest brother, Phalla, with me. The road to Pursat was severely damaged because of the war. It would take us a couple of days to get there. My mother gave me a small piece of gold for our transportation fee. She packed us food, enough for the duration of the trip. At that time, the country did not have any currency. We used gold to barter for the things we needed, including transportation. The Khmer Rouge had abolished currency in 1975.

"You take care of your little brother, you hear? Tell your brother, Samith, that we miss him and that, if he can, he should come to the city to visit us," said my mother.

"Yes, mother. I will," I responded politely.

I pressed my hands together on my chest and bowed down to say good-bye to my mother. Traditionally, pressing two hands together and bowing is a sign of respect, hello, and good-bye. That was the last time I saw my mother and my family.

This trip back to Cambodia had brought back many sad memories.

Taken in 1984 (from left to right) Phalla, Savan, Samuth, Samith
Savath, and Samoeurn (I was in the United States). Mother is in the middle.

# CHAPTER 3

# The Hard Life

The Cambodian War began in 1970 when I was in sixth grade. Our family lived in Chroy Ampil Thmey Village, along National Highway 1, approximately thirteen kilometers east of the capital, Phnom Penh. My father was a homebuilder. One of my younger brothers and I worked at my father's construction site on our days off and on school vacations to help support the family. My father worked six days a week for the construction company, while my mother stayed home, raising nine children (my two older sisters were married, and they were on their own).

My parents valued education very highly. They kept reminding us how poor we were and that only education could get us out of this poverty. My uncle bought me my first flip-flops when I was in fourth grade. Before that, I had walked to school barefoot. I played basketball barefoot, so I would not break my flip-flops. Fortunately, my brother and I did well in school, despite putting in many hours working for my father and lacking the necessary materials for school. I believed that the revolution of 1970 would give me a better opportunity to secure a higher education and, in turn, a good job. With continuous moral support from my parents, I was the only one in the village to pass the exam for a high school diploma, in 1973.

The war broke wide open that year. The Khmer Rouge successfully surrounded Phnom Penh. The Khmer Rouge occupied my school for days. Some of my classmates were drafted into the Khmer Rouge regime and others volunteered to join the Khmer Rouge combatants. Many of them were killed.

Because of the lack of safety and the need for their children to continue with school, my parents moved from the suburban Chroy Ampil Thmey Village to the capital city in the summer of 1973.

My father found a small empty space in the Center for Folklore (Leaan Prochea Prei), across from the Chamber of Marhosrop and the Faculty of Fine Arts. We built a hut in the center. One of my married sisters still lived with us, along with her daughter and her husband.

Life in the big city was difficult for us. Everything was expensive. My father had difficulty finding a job, and when he found one, the wage was very low. It was not enough to feed the family. Thankfully, there were many humanitarian organizations in the city. They provided poor people like us with food and medical care. When we got sick, we would go to the World Vision Clinic, located at the current Cambodiana Hotel, for medical care. My two younger brothers would stand in line at the CARE organization center to get a daily rice allowance. My two other brothers got up early every morning to pick up bread from the bakery to sell in the neighborhood for a small profit before school started. My brother, Samith, and I drove a cyclo (tricycle) at night and on our school holidays and days off, to make extra money to pay for our education expenses. I usually parked my cyclo in front of the hotels. European customers paid us well for the ride. One of my Khmer regular riders was an English student at one of the private schools. She was very observant when we first met.

"You are not a typical cyclo driver. Are you a detective?" she asked.

"Detective?" I chuckled. "I am not old enough to work for the government. It is wishful thinking though."

"So, who are you? What do you do for a living?" She posed more questions.

"Ma'am, you are not like my other riders. You actually try to communicate with me, the cyclo driver! I am very appreciative. However, don't you think you ask too much from a cyclo driver? This is what I do for a living." I laughed as I finished my question and response.

The woman did not give up. She pursued more questions. "From the way you look, I can see that you are not a normal cyclo driver. There are many people who have their regular jobs. They drive a cyclo to get extra income to keep up with inflation. Are you one of them?"

"Cyclo" Sam and Bonavy in Phnom Penh 1993.
I used to be cyclo taxi driver in Phnom Penh.

I began to enjoy the conversation. "You are right. Most people need to work extra to help their families. I am no different. I am a student at Tuol Svay Prey High School (formerly known as Chao Pornhea Yath). I am preparing for my first baccalaureate. My family is very poor. My parents could not afford to pay for my education, but they always remind me that I will be better off once I obtain a higher education. Driving a cyclo helps me with the school costs. Besides that, I get to learn to speak English so I can speak with my English-speaking riders. Your riding fee contributes to my education, and I thank you," I finished with a smile.

She continued, "If you like, I can teach you a couple of words every time we meet, and we can practice those words, provided that you continue to pick me up when I leave school."

"Sure!" I joyfully responded.

I was flattered to hear the offer. I enjoyed speaking with her and hoped that the ride never ended. I hoped that she was as enthusiastic as I was.

"Stop, stop here. I am home. Can you pick me up tomorrow at the same time?" she asked with a big smile.

I was more than glad to say yes.

She continued to teach me English words whenever we met. We became good friends.

*   *   *

In my spare time, I would go to the bookstore along Chrun Yu Hak Avenue near Kap Kor market to read. I read novels, storybooks, newspapers, and anything I could get my hands on. My strength was that I could retell the stories I read as if they were alive. I often made time to watch the play rehearsals at the fine arts college. Like many other teenagers, I also wanted to be a star actor or be in show business. I practiced what I saw and hoped that someday I would have a chance to perform. Life continued to be hard on us in the city.

One evening, I sat down with my parents and told them my plan. "Puk (Father) and Mear (Mother), I really want to help our family. We struggle every day to get food to feed our family. For the last couple of weeks, I've been thinking and have spoken with my cousin, Kan; he said that he could get me in the navy. I will get free food and shelter there. We can use my salary to help the family and so my brothers could continue with school. He also said that he could get me a higher officer rank once I join him."

My mother understood why I wanted to leave school. Although she left it up to my father, she had some concerns. Her only brother, who was a soldier, had been killed in combat two years earlier. She still would occasionally mourn his death.

"Are you crazy, Ah Moeurn?" (My father called me by my Cambodian name.) "I appreciate your concern and your willingness to help the family. Quitting school is not an option. As much as I want your help, I would rather see you in school getting a higher education than going to combat in this confusing war. I was a soldier for over ten years, and look where I am now. There is not a single day that I don't regret not finishing school. And look at your uncle. He was killed and left his wife and four young sons without a father. You must take your time to think about it."

His advice allowed me to put more thoughts into my plan and also offered me some comfort and reassurance. My parents repeatedly inspired me to stay in school, using education to fight poverty.

# CHAPTER 4

# Demonstration

Corruption occurred in all levels of the government. Demonstrations and protests against corruption happened daily. Most of the protesters and demonstrators were college and high school students. I was actively involved. One of the protests that I was involved in was to ask the government to release the students who were incarcerated for an unauthorized demonstration. The government had jailed them a couple of weeks earlier, charging them with disorderly conduct. The students, during a demonstration to request that the government investigate the corruption, had blocked the road. Since the country was at war, our activities were treated as a security threat to national stability. Thus, many students were arrested.

I went along with a group of students to the Ministry of Education. We asked the minister and deputy minister, Mr. Song Kim Keo and Mr. Chea Thach, to intervene and ask for the release of our fellow students. I stood in front of the ministry waiting to hear the news from the students' president, who had gone in to negotiate with the ministers. I heard the angry voice of the students' president over the megaphone, and then I saw students carrying chairs in which Mr. Song Kim Keo and Mr. Chea Thach were seated. Mr. Keo and Mr. Thach were probably in their late forties or early fifties. Mr. Keo was clean shaven and spoke in a soft tone. He tried to explain the situation to the students, but what he said did not seem to matter to anyone. Mr. Thach wore a mustache and had a short beard. He did not talk. He appeared very calm. Both ministers were cooperative. They were the nicest gentlemen in the higher ranks of government that I had witnessed.

The students put the chairs down when they reached the ground level. They asked us to hold hands and form a circle around the ministers. In that formation, we would walk toward the Independence Monument. Prior to this demonstration, Mr. Koy Pech and Mr. San That, the former students' president and vice president, had left an empty coffin to protest the kidnapping and killing of students by the government. They placed the empty coffin in the Independence Monument to perform funeral services. Many students came to join them and to pay respects. The government bought these two student leaders by offering them the rank of captain in the government force.

This time, no less than three hundred students were involved. About twenty of us held hands, forming a circle around the ministers. Although I did not know the students on either side of me, I joined hands with them. In the center of the hand circle, the ministers walked along with us. We paraded them to the west of the Independence Monument and then into "18 March" High School (formerly known as Yukunthor High School). We held the ministers on the second floor in one of the classrooms. Students took turns guarding them.

I left the demonstrators at about noon to go to lunch.

Usually, many students joined the protests, and most of the protests ended in a confrontation with government forces. I do not know what made me think that this one wouldn't end in bloodshed.

Students demanded that the government make a trade—the ministers in exchange for the incarcerated students. Instead of responding to the students' demands, the government dispatched a great number of military police (MPs) to the school. The MP units surrounded the high school. When I returned, they had closed the gate, and I was not able to get inside. Many other students were outside of the gate as well.

Many MP units began to move inside the school yard. The highest-ranking monk of the country, Reverence Venerable Huot Tat, spoke on the national radio, requesting that the students stay calm. He asked the student demonstrators to release the ministers, saying he would negotiate the release of the incarcerated students. Fearing that the venerable monk might be speaking under duress from the government, we did not honor his request. We wanted the government to guarantee the release.

I, along with many students who were outside of the gate, walked around the school, looking for an opening so we could get inside. We had no luck. The students in the school yard, who were facing the MPs, began to curse, and some of them even pushed the MPs back. Frustration had led to confrontation between the students and the MPs.

The situation became chaotic. Some students who were outside of the gate began to throw rocks. MPs swung their batons at the students. Finally, several gunshots rang out; then the sound of hundreds of rounds being fired filled the school yard. Tear gas and smoking bombs exploded in the yard. The smoke of the tear gas affected our vision. Then there were more gunshots. I felt as though we were in a war zone. I dropped to the ground, staying as low as I could, to avoid the flying bullets and rocks. The gunfire continued for about five to ten minutes. My white shirt turned brown with dirt. People were screaming and yelling. I had been next to the back gate when the gunfire began.

A Japanese reporter came out of the room where the students were keeping the ministers as hostages. She was covered with blood. She had been shot in the shoulder. She told us that the ministers had been assassinated by "a person unknown." I was shocked and scared. She described the gunman as tall and thin, wearing a black shirt and blue jeans. I looked around for the person matching this description. I was furious, upset, and confused. I thought that, if we, the students, had not acted so foolishly, these nice ministers probably would still be alive.

The government quickly announced the murder of the ministers. They claimed that the Khmer Rouge took the opportunity during the chaotic moment to kill the ministers.

I went home after the chaotic events, and my brother-in-law told me to stay away from activities outside of school. "You should only be focused on schoolwork," he said.

# CHAPTER 5

# The Evacuations

Beginning in January 1975, Khmer Rouge rockets flew into the capital almost daily. The Communists were close to capturing the city. Bombs exploded very often, especially in crowded places like movie theaters or public markets. Hospitals were filled with injured soldiers and civilians. One day, I was driving my cyclo close to where a rocket fell in front of Monorom Hotel, next to Phnom Pech movie theatre. I parked my cyclo to dodge the debris. When all the debris had settled and it appeared safe, I pushed my cyclo forward to see the victims. The hit location was surrounded by police. After they took the victims out, I found a silver locket in the shape of a fish soaked with blood. I picked it up and took it home. I washed it and gave to my little sister.

The whole city was in chaos. Protesters turned against the government, and sometimes these conflicts ended in bloody fights. Faith in the government continued to fade. General Lon Nol, paralyzed by a stroke, could not be an effective leader. As the government forces weakened, the American Embassy staff was ordered to withdraw. I will never forget the day that the marine helicopters came to evacuate the Americans. It was April 12, 1975. I saw many helicopters circling the buildings close to where I lived. Out of curiosity, I went out to take a look. The gate of the building was closed. The helicopters landed one by one to drop off the American soldiers. The marines spread around the perimeter of the building to protect their interests. I leaned on the bars of the fence, observing the activities. Foreigners, as well as Cambodians with big suitcases, ran to the helicopters. These privilege Cambodians were those who worked for the American Embassy, were family members of high-ranking officers, or had American spouses.

It was the first time I had seen African American soldiers. I kept staring at one of them, wondering about his teeth. "Look at his teeth. They are extremely white," I said to the other teenager who stood next to me.

I was impressed with the military equipment he had. I attempted to converse with him in my broken English.

He looked at me and smiled, "How are you doing?"

I was so happy that he had spoken to me. I responded with joy in my voice, "I am nineteen years old, thank you."

He continued to speak to me with a sincere smile. "Would you like to come with us?" he asked.

I do not know if he was serious or just joking with me. I took a long pause, thinking to myself. *Go with them?* It seemed like the war would soon be over. Why would I want to leave? Besides, I did not know where he would take me, and if our destination was America, how would I survive in the big country? Did they have rice to eat there? What about my family? Who would I live with?

These crazy thoughts ran through my head for a minute before I politely responded, "I cannot go. My family is here. My country will be at peace. I don't want to leave my family."

He nodded his head, smiling. I watched the helicopters as they went up and down retrieving their passengers. I waved good-bye to the soldiers and left the scene only after all the helicopters were gone. I went home to tell my family about the departure of the American Embassy staff, saying that the war would soon be over. We should be able to live in peace again.

The night of April 16, the city was so quiet that you could hear a mosquito buzz. The city had always imposed the curfew at 9:00 p.m. But that night, it was quite unusually silent. There was no sound of rockets or gunshots. It seemed that the government had dispatched all of its soldiers and military police to the street. They were quietly patrolling the streets and buildings. They were in military uniforms, equipped with armor. I noticed that many of them wore civilian clothes underneath their uniforms. I couldn't help but ask one of the soldiers who was patrolling the building near where I lived, "What is going on? Is there going to be fighting in the city?"

He looked at me with sadness in his eyes. "We lost the war. I fear for my life. We will face the uncertainty of the new regime. I battled with the Khmer Rouge before and was captured and taken into their zone. I remember how cruelly they treated us. I was fortunate to escape. They were known to kill their own people without mercy. Most of their soldiers are children who pulled the triggers for fun. I do not trust them," he murmured.

I listened to him with concern, but it disappeared quickly when I thought of the upcoming peace—no more war! I went back to bed with a smile and dreamed of my bright future.

I woke up very early to the noises of celebration on April 17, 1975. I found many soldiers' uniforms on the ground. I looked behind my hut to witness the Mekong River turning black. It was filled with Khmer Rouge soldiers swimming toward the capital. These Khmer Rouge units who first arrived took control of the military tanks and trucks. They paraded on the streets of Phnom Penh. Government forces did not put up much of a fight. They simply surrendered. With the fear of being retaliated against, many soldiers took off their uniforms and welcomed the Khmer Rouge. White flags, as a sign of surrender, were everywhere. We heard that the government's generals were rounded up at the Olympic Stadium. They congratulated the Khmer Rouge for their victory.

Most Cambodians felt relief. An estimate of five hundred thousand Cambodians had died during the five years of war. We thought the war was over. Many began to make plans to rejoin family members from whom they had been separated during the war. Looters broke into stores and started to loot just a few hours later. They took whatever they could get their hands on.

One of the Khmer Rouge soldiers, a middle-aged man, told us that he came from the east side of the country, my mother's hometown. He asked me to go with him to get some cigarettes. I told him where he could find the cigarettes. I did not want to leave my family during the chaotic time. He nodded his head. Then he took our family's motorcycle and left. I thought that we would never see our motorcycle again. A few minutes later, he came back with hundreds of packs of cigarettes. He again asked me to go with him to pick up some goods. I told him that I still did not want to leave my family, and I offered to drop him off anywhere he wanted to go in Phnom Penh city. He was upset but surprisingly understanding.

I drove him and dropped him off at the New Market. I thanked him for the cigarettes he gave to my father.

On my way back home, I saw people carrying televisions and boxes of goods. Some people fought over the things that they wanted to take. I tried not to participate in these anarchist activities. I drove my motorcycle to the street along the Tonle Sap River, where the traffic was less heavy. I looked into the river, basking in the many dreams in my head. I dreamed of peace and freedom. I saw myself riding on my bike to school and playing sports. I saw laughter among families and friends. I saw our family celebrating a reunion with my grandmother, who we had not seen since the war started four years earlier. I saw myself, having succeeded in school, with a dream job.

All of these dreams disappeared quickly when I heard the gunshots. A Khmer Rouge soldier, who appeared to be one of the commanders, pointed a pistol into the sky, ordering mass evacuation. People ran like schools of fish. I stopped and walked my bike to the side of the road in front of the Langka Temple. The Khmer Rouge soldier with the portable microphone kept repeating the announcement, "The American aggressors will drop bombs on the capital in retaliation for their loss. You must leave the city as quickly as you can. You may come back in three days."

I took this message seriously. I went home and told my family what I had heard, and we made a plan to leave the city.

Only a few roads exited the city. Two to three million people were to evacuate the capital. Heeding the Khmer Rouge scare tactic and in fear that American B-52 bombers would retaliate, people hurriedly headed out of the city unprepared. The Khmer Rouge ordered all hospitals to evacuate their staff as well as their patients. Khmer Rouge soldiers entered the hospitals and killed the wounded government soldiers and suspected soldiers.

It would take about a week to clear people from the capital city. Many would lose their lives along the way because of disease and lack of medical care.

Our family was large. Both of my sisters came to our place to discuss the plan. Between the two of them, they had five young daughters. My parents still had nine of us living at home. Altogether, there were twenty of us. I was the oldest son in the family with the highest education. I had been preparing for my first baccalaureate before the collapse of the government. I was considered by my family to have the better judgment. That meant that I would make a lot of decisions for the family. We made a definite plan that we would meet at my father's hometown, Chroy Ampil. We would stay at my uncle's house, about thirteen kilometers from the city, for the few days before we were allowed to come back to Phnom Penh.

I took my two little brothers, Pich and Duke, with me on my father's motorcycle. The traffic getting out of Phnom Penh, especially on Monivong's bridge, was congested. It took us more than two hours to get to our uncle's house. We stayed there waiting for other family members to arrive. We saw many evacuees passing by; none were our family members. I started to worry.

I left my brothers at my uncle's home and walked around to gather information and to observe the current situation. I saw many cars that had run out of gas on the sidewalk, as well as in the middle of the road. Some vehicle owners traded their cars for pulling carts to keep their family moving. They put their elders, youngsters, and their few valuable personal belongings on the carts. Before I realized where I was, I had already walked as far back as three kilometers. I took a rest in the unmerciful heat of April. I glared around, looking for my family. I was very happy to see my schoolmate, Dok. We began to talk about the current events and the endless possibilities of getting a job after we finished school this year. We were eager to serve the country in this newly formed government. We went our separate ways when night came.

My family arrived two days later. On their way out of Phnom Penh, they'd had to stop at several places to pick up food and necessary items. They also complained that the traffic was terrible to navigate, even with the pulling cart that they had.

My uncle's home was built above the ground. There was a bamboo bed underneath the house to accommodate guests. The adults would socialize as they would sit around the bamboo bed playing chess, while we kids played outside. My mother prepared food for us. After we ate, we went around the neighborhood to greet our extended relatives. There were many of us to fit on the bamboo bed. My mother rolled out a mat made of palm tree on the ground. We rested there for the night.

Typical Cambodian Home (1997);
(From left to right) Khay Touch, Phalla, and the neighbors (whose names I
have forgotten)

# CHAPTER 6

# The Beginning of the Struggle

After a week of evacuation, we ran out of food and supplies. I went to Dok's home in Prek Ta Koy. Dok's sister prepared us lunch. Dok's sister told us that many people had gone back into the city to find food. They'd found many stockpiles of rice. She told us where the rice warehouse was.

After the meal, Dok and I swam across the Mekong River to the city to look for rice. We went to a huge warehouse where the government stocked rice. People ran in and came out with bags of rice. Dok and I looked around to see if there were any Khmer Rouge soldiers. We hurried to the warehouse once the coast was clear.

Inside were mountains of rice bags. Since the top of the pile was too high to reach, people only pulled the bags that were stacked underneath. Mountains of rice bags collapsed on people. No one had enough mercy to rescue anyone. Everyone had to be quick to get out before the soldiers came to arrest or, worse, kill us. Instead of helping the fallen victims, the crowd ignored the outcries of suffering, and people stepped on whoever was trapped beneath the bags. I wanted to make sure that I did not walk on those who were trapped.

Dok and I built a raft that could carry about five hundred pounds of rice. We took turns running to the warehouse to get bags of rice to place on the raft. By the time we got back to Dok's home, it was dark. We told Dok's sister of how we'd found the rice warehouse and all the activities in the warehouse. We were glad that we were safe and were able to bring some rice home. After dinner, I loaded the bags on my motorcycle to bring to my family. I imagined that all the rice I had collected would last us a month at least. We hoped that the Khmer Rouge would let us come back home and return to our daily routine before we finished our rice supply. Sadly, we were very mistaken.

Inflation skyrocketed. One bag of rice cost fifty times more than it had the week before. My mother had not seen so much money in her life. When she found out about the current price for a bag of rice, she managed to sell two of them. She told me not to worry. "It is much easier to carry the money than bags of rice," she said. "I am sure that the new government will let us back home soon." My mother exchanged some of the leftover rice for salt, sugar, fish, meat, and vegetables. She also exchanged some of it for medicine for my family.

Unfortunately, the Khmer Rouge abolished the use of money and declared everything the property of the organization or, as they called it, the Angkar. People were also the property of the Angkar. We were not allowed to eat our homegrown fruit and vegetables. Everyone would receive food through the Angkar distribution. Whoever got caught stealing food would be severely punished.

People were divided into two groups—"the old people" and "the new people." The old people were those who had been living under Khmer Rouge control before April 1975. They had full rights and could join the party or military. They received better food distribution. More importantly, they were the rulers of the second group. The rest, including our family, had no rights. The new people were not trustworthy, and they were on execution lists. I called us the "slaves of the war."

Within this rank, there were categories that determined whether an individual would simply be sent to work as a slave-laborer, starved and worked to death, or subjected to immediate execution. New people who were sick and not able to go to work in the rice field would not receive their food allowance. The rationale was that "sick people are not hungry." Let me remind the reader that most of the sickness during the Khmer Rouge regime was because of hunger, fatigue, and excessive hours of daily work without enough nutrition.

People who refused to cooperate with the rules would be executed. The Khmer Rouge often tested people to confirm their loyalty to the Angkar. They would order the father to kill the son or vice versa. If someone refused to follow the order, everyone involved would be killed.

The Khmer Rouge closed all the schools in the country. When the schools were reopened a year later, they offered first and second grade (at least in my area). Most of the students were the old people's children. The new people's children were sent to the rice fields to work. The Khmer Rouge used fear tactics, torture, and killing to retain control and remain in power.

# CHAPTER 7

# Desperation

My father and I built a hut on our land along National Route 1. We barely had enough palm leaves to cover the roof. July and August were the rainy season. We often sat up all night when it rained. Even with the lack of sleep, the Khmer Rouge expected us to be in the rice field the next morning. They provided us with little food to eat. We had to use our leftover rice to supplement our needs. After two months, we ran out of extra rice. Everyone was hungry, weary, and irritable.

I asked my parents to allow me to sneak back into the city to get food. They feared for my life and did not let me go. I told them that I knew where the rice was and that, if I got caught, I would have to accept the consequences. My parents begged me not to take the chance. "You could be killed, you know?" my mother cried.

Out of desperation, I asked for permission to go to West River, the hometown of my brother-in-law, Sareth, to search for food. It was about a twenty-five-kilometer walk. The region was known to have lots of corn, peanuts, jacamars, and fruit. My parents allowed me to go, provided that I take my younger brother along for company. Samith and I left without asking the permission of the village chief. "I will take care of him," said my father. The chief of the village was my father's cousin's son. At the time, the rules were not strictly enforced.

Samith and I took the back road to West River. We had to go through Doan Sar Temple. Then we swam across Big Lake and continued walking for another twelve kilometers. We saw many bodies along the way. The Khmer Rouge were rounding up the former government soldiers and killing them. We could hear the gunshots and sometimes the fearful cries of the victims. We pretended that there was nothing going on and kept on walking. The other side of the lake was the land that the Khmer Rouge had captured in 1973. It was green with vegetation. We arrived at Brother Samon's home just before dark. Brother Samon and his family were among the "old people."

Brother Samon was the eldest brother of my brother-in-law, Sareth. He was married and had five children. His eldest son, Samun, was about three years younger than me. Samun, Chanthan (Samun's cousin), and I used to hang out in the rice fields and take care of the cows. Brother Samon was always a farmer, before and after the war. He was a good fisherman, and he owned land and a herd of cows. He was very pleased to see us. I told him that his brother could not make it because my sister, Savath, was just having another girl. Brother Samon welcomed his second niece, Savath's second daughter. He was concerned about his brother's well-being. He appeared secretive when he spoke to me. He asked me to ask his brother to bring his family to live with him when I returned. While his wife prepared dinner for us, we chatted about the old times. He told me about Chanthan, his nephew. Chanthan was one of my best friends.

"Chanthan joined the revolution force to fight back against the government. He was killed last year in a fight," said Brother Samon.

I had many fond memories of Chanthan. I remember his athletic ability. Chanthan could ride standing up on a cow's back while the cow was running without falling off. He could swim and run quickly. He was a good fisherman. His eyes were sharp. He could spot beehives far away and could quickly gather the honey and hive for dessert. There were so many other special abilities that I saw in him, and I had learned much from him. Chanthan was strong and fearless. I was sad to hear that he had passed.

As "old people," Brother Samon and his family had more food supplies and freedom than we did. He and his wife packed up as much food as we could carry to bring home. My brother and I were able to bring back corn, rice, and dried fish for the family.

In our region, the Angkar began to restrict travelling around starting in August 1975. The food rations we were getting were smaller and smaller. None of us would be able to travel to West River to get help. We were hungry all the time. With the continuous scarcity of food, our family often had arguments and conflicts. I found that my father was upset with us almost all the time. A chain-smoker, he was irritable because of nicotine withdrawal. He would scream at us for not being able to assist him in finding extra food or get him tobacco and tobacco-like leaves (generic leaves).

During midday break, my brother and I would go into the jungle, searching for hidden ponds to fish. People could get injured or even killed while looking for ponds. There were many dud munitions left on the ground after the war. People often accidently stepped on the munitions or chopped them with the shovels, causing them to explode. Most ponds had been discovered and were fished out. One time, we found a small pond that had not been touched. My brother and I built a levy and emptied one side to catch the fish. We got many water snakes out of that pond, instead of fish. We were lucky that those snakes were not poisonous.

My father complained that I was too honest, not able to find a way to get ahead in this new regime, and that I would not survive the Angkar's revolution. He told me to steal the Angkar's rice, fruit, meat, corn, and tobacco. Everyone knew the Angkar's rule; if you stole and got caught, you would be killed on the spot. I told my father that I'd rather die of hunger than be shot for stealing. He screamed at me, "I don't want to see your face again, ever." He probably did not mean that, but hearing such unexpected words from a loved one did hurt.

I told my mother that we should go to Battambang, the west side of the country, where the most rice was planted. I was sure that we would not be hungry once we got there. In addition, the Angkar transported many of the new people by boat to the west. We would not have to worry about of how we would get there. My mother discussed this with my father, and they decided not to go and to stay close to Phnom Penh. "Battambang is too far from the city. If they open the city, it would take weeks for us to reach Phnom Penh," said my father. My parents still believed that the Angkar would let us go back.

I felt hopeless and helpless watching my family's suffering, my father's pain from nicotine withdrawal, and my little brothers and sister crying out for food. I was upset and angry with myself for not being able to comfort them. Anxiety, depression, and hunger had been weakening my immune system. I finally caught a violent fever.

I was chilled. My body shook. In Cambodia, it did not matter what kind of illness you had; the first defense was to get a body massage by coining. Usually, a relative would use the coin with oil, sometime kerosene, to massage your body. They would coin you along the ribs until your skin turned red. If you were very sick, the color of the skin that was coined would turn dark brown.

All my family went out to work in the rice fields; only my twelve-year-old sister was home. She coined me. I clenched my teeth as I lay facing down on the mat to make it easier for her to coin my back. I was angry with our current situation. I felt helpless for not being able to help my family. I screamed to let out my frustration. I guess I scared my little sister. She dropped the coin on my back and ran for help. She told people that I was possessed by an evil spirit. The next thing I knew, Savan got sick from being startled and scared.

I felt that I had let my family down and that I should not be an additional burden to them. I told Samith and Samuth, my younger brothers, that I planned to run away. They begged to come along. That night, we walked about twelve miles to West River to wait for the boat to go to Battambang Province. We spent two nights at Koh Kra Bey's riverbank, in front of the Pagoda Temple. Surprisingly, my mother and my brother in-law found us. My mother told me that she had found my good-bye note and suspected that I might be here, since I had talked a lot about going west.

My mother sat next to me and looked up to the sky as she talked. "I understand how you feel. It is very hard to live under this unmerciful regime. But you know that we love you; your father loves you. His outburst is a result of his frustration. You can understand that, right? He is used to being the sole supporter of the family. It must be very difficult for him not to be able to do that."

Yes, my mother was right. My father was the breadwinner, a strong man who had vowed to support and protect his family. This Angkar thing did not allow him to be the father he once had been.

My mother continued, "Whatever conflicts we have within our family, we need to talk about them and resolve them. I ask that you come back home. You and your brothers are the older sons. Your father and I believe that you will be able to take care of your younger brothers and sisters after we pass on. If you strongly believe that we should go to the west, then we must go together, as a family." She continued, giving me several reasons why we should hang tight.

I was moved by my mother's speech. I felt so overwhelmed that my eyes filled with tears. Finally, I held her hand, and we cried together.

\*     \*     \*

"Are you okay honey?" My wife shook my shoulder.

"What happed?" I asked.

My wife told me that I was crying in my sleep. She asked if I wanted something to eat.

I asked her to ask the flight attendant to bring us some juice. I closed my eye to rest after the drink.

I realized that I was caught up in the past. I remembered that I had returned home with my mother after our long cry and my apology to my mother. "Mother," I promised, "I will not do this again, and I will try to be a good son."

# CHAPTER 8

# Khmer Rouge Deception

The rainy season had fully arrived in August 1975. Our hut barely withstood the rain and wind. We could see stars through our roof. The rain kept us awake at night, leaving us exhausted, but we had to work the next day to get our food ration. We became hostile and hardly spoke to one another.

One morning, my second cousin, the chief of the village, asked all the evacuees to attend a meeting.

A man dressed in the Khmer Rouge military uniform spoke on the portable microphone. "I have good news. The city is safe now. In order to rebuild our country, the Angkar needs former government employees, teachers, businessmen, engineers, electricians, students, and intellectuals to return to the capital."

The Khmer Rouge claimed that they were prepared to bring us back into the city. In order to facilitate the transportation, the Angkar requested that we enlist ourselves. There was a form where we would give information, such as our names, education, and employment experience. "Angkar wants you!" the military man shouted.

The man claimed that the Angkar would protect us from the American bombers and that it was not possible for the Americans to harm us. The Angkar was ready to put educators, engineers, business leaders, royal descendants, and those who were intellects to work.

I couldn't stop smiling. I was so excited about this news. *I am glad that they finally realized that they could not run the country without the help of intellectuals*, I thought to myself. I had previously believed that the Angkar had no interest in foreign relationships or valued educators. *I was wrong!* People had experienced the lack of food after only four months of living by the Angkar's food allowance. I was glad that the regime had finally realized that being independent from foreign aid or trade was wrong. This is what I understood after I heard the announcement on the megaphone.

We had a family meeting that evening to discuss whether we should sign up to go. My father was very skeptical about the Khmer Rouge. He reminded us of the three-day promise that had become four months. "We have been in this situation before. The Angkar is very tricky. They have not proved to be trustworthy. As you can see and have heard, they killed so many people. They hold a strong grudge against 'new people' like us. I just don't trust them," said my father.

I was anxious. My father's reluctance to return to Phnom Penh irritated me. "Father, the Angkar gives us the opportunity to rebuild our lives, our country. I will have the chance to go back to finish school and to be able to support our family. You should consider this offering." I told him that whether the family agreed to sign up or not, I definitely wanted to go with the Khmer Rouge to Phnom Penh.

My mother was concerned about the breaking up of the family. She was able to convince my father to sign up, since she did not want to lose us again. She feared that the family could never be one again if my father refused to go. We went to the temple, Watt Champa, to enlist. After the registration, the Angkar asked us to go back to pack up our belongings and wait for transportation at the temple. They kept us on the waiting list and told us that we would leave in about two days. We were not allowed to leave the temple after we had registered. We had brought all we needed from our temporary shelter. We received a food distribution daily from the Angkar while waiting.

The first night, my second cousin, who worked for the Khmer Rouge, came to speak with my father. "Uncle, I do not think it is a good idea for you to leave. I heard some bad news. I don't know what it is, but I know it is bad."

"As you know, once I've enrolled, I can't get out. I have to go," my father told him.

"I know people, and I can get you out," said my cousin.

My father considered doing so, but I was strongly opposed. "Father, I will not go back. I am going to leave, with or without you," I told him.

Because he had so much love for his children, my father decided to stay with us. The moving trucks came to pick us up on the second day. As I recall, there were more than twenty trucks that day. Each truck loaded twenty to twenty-five passengers. The Angkar made us throw away our belongings and anything that we carried. "Comrade, Angkar has planned everything for you. A place to live and plenty of food will be yours upon your arrival," the regime promised.

The trucks began to move out of Watt Champa. We smiled and waved good-bye as the trucks departed from our temporary shelter. "Good-bye, hunger; hello, new life," I whispered.

Some people were happy; others, like my father, were concerned and ambivalent. The trucks moved slowly into the capital. We clapped our hands as the trucks went over the Monivong's bridge. I pointed to the warehouse where Dok and I had found rice a few months earlier for my family. The trucks kept moving forward, passing the Royal Palace and then the Old Market. In front of Langka temple, I saw many loaded trucks dumping books in the river. I began to worry about where we would end up. People in my truck tried to guess where the Khmer Rouge would drop us off. They had fun with the guessing game. However, they had to change their guesses many times, as it seemed the truck driver did not have any intention of stopping.

Before we knew it, the truck was headed out of the city and was westbound. We looked at each other with fear. Some people in my truck cried out; others wept. We knew the Angkar had lied to us again. The Khmer Rouge, who were escorting the truck, raised their AK-47s, ready to shoot anyone who dared jump off the truck. They stared coldly at us, without speaking a word. The road had many potholes caused by lack of maintenance and the last five years of war. We rocked and rolled, thrown up and down as the truck hit many of those holes. The unstable motion of the truck made Savath and her six-month-old baby very sick. We often heard gunshots from other trucks. People must have been trying to escape. I was speechless. My face was wet with tears. I feared for my family's lives. The Khmer Rouge was known for its hatred of the city people, the intellectuals, and the rich. These evacuees had provided their families' background information, which made lying out of the question. I thought that, if we lied, they would know. We would be put on the top of their execution lists. I deeply regretted not listening to my father. I felt that I was to blame for this. I should have listened to my father and my cousin. My father did not say a word to me.

The trucks stopped when it was dark, before we reached Kampong Chhnang Province (about eighty kilometers from Phnom Penh.) Our two escort soldiers rounded us up about eight meters from the truck. They told us that they would not hesitate to shoot anyone who tried to escape. Then, they gave us rice and dried fish to cook.

While preparing dinner, Sareth told us to burn anything that could identify who we were, including family photos and identification cards. Except for Savath and her baby, who cried nonstop, we quickly fell asleep after the dinner due to exhaustion. Just as my niece calmed down and Savath was going to take her first rest, the noises of gunshots sounded. It scared my little niece. She began to cry again and did not stop crying for the whole night. We assumed that someone must have been shot for trying to escape. We prayed that we would not get hit by the bullets.

The Khmer Rouge woke us up just before sunrise. "Get in the truck," the soldiers ordered. "We need to move."

The trucks moved very slowly due to the road conditions. We stopped at Kra Kor for lunch. We continued the trip for the next six hours before we reached our final destination. Some people managed to escape during the trip. We could not do so even if we thought about it. Our family of sixteen was too large to move around without notice.

We arrived in the city of Pursat at night.

# CHAPTER 9

# Green Land

Pursat Province was the fourth-largest province in Cambodia. It was located in the western part of the country and bordered, clockwise from the north, Battambang Province, the Tonle Sap, Kampong Chhnang Province, Kampong Speu Province, Koh Kong Province, and Thailand. It was located between the Tonle Sap and the northern end of the Cardamom Mountains. The Pursat River bisected the province, running from the Cardamoms in the west to the Tonle Sap in the east. Pursat was accessible by National Highway 5, by boat, by rail, and by numerous smaller roads. Pursat Province was about 186 kilometers northwest of Phnom Penh by road and 106 kilometers southeast of Battambang. The province was known to have good land for plantations and a lake for fishing. I believed that, if they did not kill us, we would at least not go hungry anymore. They would prove me wrong again.

We felt a bit of relief when the Khmer Rouge told us that this was our final destination. After we got off the truck, my brother-in-law found logs to prepare the fire for cooking. There were many coconut trees along the street and in the yards. We went in to pick up coconuts and young coconuts to eat. It was the first time in nearly five months since we'd had anything good to eat.

When we were about to take a rest, we heard the buffalo carts and the sound of the buffalo bells. I wandered out to take a look. There were hundreds of buffalo carts coming. The drivers did not unhitch the buffalo from the cart to give them a rest. Instead, they walked around, looking at the families who had just been dropped off by the trucks. This reminded me of a book I read about the history of American slavery. When the Spaniards and the Englishmen brought the Africans to America, the farm owners went around looking for

34

the healthiest slaves to buy. I snooped to listen to their conversation. I heard their discussion of which families would be good for their village. I ran back to my family. None of us knew anything about the Pursat Province area, except from what we had read. This was the first time any of us had ever been in that province. There was no reason for us to try to please any of the cart drivers. As a result, we were almost the last family to be picked.

The long line of buffalo carts rolled out of Srok Kandeang. The carts were pulled through mud in the rainy season. The drivers constantly used the whip on their buffalo to encourage them to pull harder. We walked behind the cart. Only women with small children and the elderly were allowed to ride on the cart. Savath, Savan, Ravy, and the baby were in the cart, along with our few belongings. The drivers took us to a very remote area.

The water supply was always the main problem in the village where we were placed. People who lived there would go weeks without bathing in the summer. In the autumn, the village would be flooded with rain.

Each new people's family was adopted by a family of the old people. It was after midnight when we got to Phum Thmey, our new village. We slept on the ground that night. The next morning, the chief of the village gathered all the new people and asked them to provide their family background in writing. We did not question them, even though we knew that we had given them this information before we got on the truck in Watt Champa. Questioning them could result in our deaths. I persuaded my family to tell the truth. I told my family that whatever we said before we got on the truck had to be consistent with what we told them now. Families who did not tell the truth would later be arrested and would disappear. Of course we did not know this at the time.

I guess we were very lucky. The family who adopted us was very kind. They helped us build a hut behind their home. In addition to the Angkar's food allowance, they often gave us rice to supplement our needs. Savath was still weak and was on bed rest until the harvest season. Her baby was not quite six months old when she died of malnutrition and lack of medicine.

# CHAPTER 10

# Reeducation Camp

During the first year of the Khmer Rouge ruling, our family suffered only one loss, my niece.

The Angkar reduced our allowance to a small bowl of porridge, which consisted of a half spoon of rice and the rest water, twice daily. The Khmer Rouge immediately sent us to work in the rice fields. We had to work over sixteen hours per day. The soldiers executed people who complained about work. We could not even comment on the food to say that it was too little, too salty, or tasteless. Anyone who dared to speak would likely be killed.

Everyone whose lives had been spared was still under investigation. Teenagers were sent to reeducation camps. Samith and I were sent to different classes at the headquarters in Kandeang Village to be reeducated. The Angkar had us make a shed to sleep in, in the school yard. They fed us a very small daily ration. We were starving. The soup they made for us on the first night had some kind of vegetable in it that made our throat itch. Many of us scratched our necks until they bled. Those who complained about the food were taken away. We all thought the Khmer Rouge had brought us here to find a better excuse to kill us.

The Khmer Rouge leaders taught us the vision of the Angkar and what the regime would do to accomplish the plan. They openly informed us that whoever got in the way of the Angkar would be killed. "They are enemies of the people; they must be killed," they bluntly said.

The Khmer Rouge encouraged us to provide constructive ideas for development of the country. Teenagers who raised their hands to offer a different approach toward development of the Angkar's movement disappeared nightly from the camp. Samith and I learned not to speak up and to adopt a "yes, sir" attitude to survive. We began with about two hundred teenagers in the camp; by the end of the week, about thirty of us had disappeared. We had no doubt that those who disappeared were executed for exercising free speech.

The Khmer Rouge celebrated the closing of reeducation camp with unlimited Cambodian noodle soup. We had not seen this much food since the fall of the Kampuchea Republic. All the teenagers and I ate and ate like there would be no tomorrow. I wanted to keep as much of the food in my stomach as I could for as long as I could. I ate so much that I thought I was going to die from not being able to breathe. Many threw up from overeating.

After the reeducation camp, the Khmer Rouge began to execute former soldiers and teachers. The green land became the killing fields.

# CHAPTER 11

# Survival Skills

Life in the village was still a struggle when we came back. Many people who had come with us from Phnom Penh had been killed. The living were on their way to the grave. People had to find other sustenance to supplement their daily nutrition. My adopted family ran out of their rice stock and was suffering the same fate as we were. They generously taught us how to fish and to identify edible plants in the woods. They did as much as they could to save us.

My father taught me an important lesson that kept me alive during the holocaust. One day, my father, Samith, and I went fishing. We found a pond where buffalo soaked to keep from burning in the sun. We saw many fish swimming up and down, trying to get some fresh air above the muddy water. We built a small dam across the pond. It took us at least a couple hours to empty the pond and catch the fish. We were happy to see so many fish rolling and trying to hide in the mud after all the water went to the other side of the dam.

"Moeurn, there is a big leech under your crotch!" my brother screamed.

I looked down; used my hand to feel between my legs; and yes, it was a big leech. I jumped across the dam, breaking it and causing the water to flow back to the empty side, where the catchable fish had been. I have to admit that I had always been frightened of being bitten by leeches before this. I crawled up on the grass, rolled around, and screamed for help. Samith was much braver than I was. He pulled the leech off my leg and threw it out. My father was angry. It was dark now, and we had lost most of the fish that we were going to catch.

"Son, let me tell you, leeches don't kill you; starvation and the Khmer Rouge kill you," said my father angrily.

Throughout my life, my father had given me many bits of advice; this turned out to be one of the best. It made everything else irrelevant if I wanted to survive. His words saved my life. Now I knew my fate. I was there to be killed. If I wanted to live, I had to summon my inner strength; only if I did so could I fight this bad fate and survive. I pledged to myself that I would stay alive during this horrific period of life. When I was in the rice fields with my adopted family, I would pay close attention so that I could learn to farm rice. I became one of the fastest farmers in pulling and planting rice. My adopted family was pleased with my improvement.

While we waited for the harvest season, there was a period during which the work in the rice field was slow. The food allowances were smaller, since we did not work as much as we had during the plantation time. To supplement our needs, we were given a trapping net called "morng" to catch fish. I spread the morng in the rice fields to trap fish. I got fish, freshwater crabs, and snakes. Those water snakes were not poisonous, but they were wild and mean. I was bit many times. I did not care about the snakes; nor was I bothered by leeches' bites at all.

The harvest season arrived. Equipped with new skills, I cut and separated rice grain from the stem.

I was placed in the teenagers' group. Comrade Oeun was my group leader. She did not like new people. She thought that new people were lazy and did not want to work hard for the Angkar and she could not tolerate their ignorance. I felt that she was snobby and was sitting on a high horse. However, her skills at harvesting were uncompromised. I watched her work as she collected rice stems and tied them into bundles.

I did not do well for the first few weeks, but before the harvest season was over, I was able to harvest as fast as she could. I was placed in a special harvest group because of my speed. Most teenagers in this group were among the old people. In this group, we received better meals. I was very happy that my hard work was paying off. I continued to increase my farming skills.

When the harvest season was over, the Angkar sent the teenagers out of town to dig a canal to improve irrigation. Their claim was that we would be able to harvest three times a year and have plenty of rice for people to eat. I was sent to the southwest of my village, about fifteen kilometers away from home.

We were sent to work under the burning heat of the April, May, and June sun. The leaders divided us into several groups of twelve to fifteen, each group with a group leader. Three groups made a section with a section leader. All group leaders were old people. In addition to the group leaders, a couple of young Khmer Rouge soldiers watched us. These child soldiers did not need much reason to kill. Not only did we work under the hot sun, we worked in front of a cannon.

I liked to entertain my group by telling stories during short breaks to reduce the boredom. My stories ranged from romance to action to horror to comedy. One day, a soldier passed by and found me telling a kung fu story. With my stick that I utilized for carrying the dirt baskets out to the trench, I performed some kung fu moves as the story progressed. To my surprise, the soldier liked my story. When we returned to camp, he asked me to meet him in his shed.

"Can you tell me the story you told your comrades today?" he asked.

"Sure, Comrade Sok," I responded with a smile.

I had learned many stories from school and from books that I read. I also had seen many kung fu movies. It would be easy for me to tell stories, as long as I did not get killed. He was happy to hear that I had agreed to tell him stories.

Comrade Sok allowed me to sleep in his mosquito net to continue telling the stories nightly. As a result, I was fed better and was able to sleep without getting bit by mosquitoes. In July, I became ill. I had an infection on my crotch where the leech had bitten me. I had difficult moving and was constantly in pain. Comrade Sok was worried. He asked his nurse to take care of the infection. The teenager nurse was very shy and reluctant to treat me. He hardly gave me any medication for the pain. The good thing that came out of this was that he believed that I was in pain. Comrade Sok ordered the nurse to send me to the district's hospital. Since the hospital was about fifteen to twenty kilometers away and I was not able to walk that far, Comrade Sok gave me a ride on his bike.

The district hospital had been built in the middle of the woods and bamboo bushes. It had no more than ten staff members. To my knowledge, the hospital served at least five villages, including

Phum Thmey, Phum Thlea Ampil, Phum Por, Phum Porpee, and Phum Preah Theat Temple. Most new people who were sent to the hospital were likely to die for lack of medicine, poorly trained staff, and poor health care. Likely, none of the staff members knew anything about Western medicine. They treated patients with herbal medicines.

When Comrade Sok dropped me off at the hospital, instead of telling the nurse of my problem, he said that I was a great storyteller and that the nurse would enjoy my company. Though there was no medication to relive my pain, I was fed well in the hospital. I was given a black and brown substance to put on my crotch and was told to wash myself every day. I became the storyteller for the hospital staff. My wound did not get any better.

One morning, when I woke up, I saw an old man with gray hair and a blue sweater beside my bed. He looked sad. I blinked my eyes a few times before I recognized my father. He looked very old.

"Puk, how did you get here?" My head was racing. How had my father known that I was here? I had not wanted my family to know that I was ill. I had wanted to take care of myself while they focused their energy on taking care of themselves.

My father told me that the teenagers' camp had been disbanded. All the teenagers had returned to the village to help plant rice. Samith had told him that I'd been sent to the hospital for an illness, but my brother had not known the type of illness I had. My father appeared extremely worried about my health. He told me that, after he had heard the news, he'd asked his leader if he could visit me. He'd brought me rice that he'd gathered from parts of my siblings' allowances and dried fish. He had walked through woods, slippery mud, and ponds to get to where I stayed. His pants were still wet, and there was still some mud on his back and waist. It looked like he had fallen down on his way here.

I was overwhelmed with love, excitement, and affection for my father. My eyes were teary. I assured him that I was okay; it was just an infection, and it should be healed soon. I told him that the wound had been caused by the leech when we'd emptied the pond for the fish that summer. We both laughed. It was a huge relief. He nodded his head, "Yes, I remember. You jumped out of the pond with the leech on your crotch. I was mad." He talked with a smile.

41

I asked my father to go ahead and eat the rice that he'd brought for me, as I had plenty of food here. I asked the nurse to bring me food so that I could have lunch with my father. My father was relieved to see me in good health, except for the infection. He told me how everyone was doing at the village. He said that the family would be so happy to hear that I was not seriously ill.

"You are the luckiest kid I've known. Look at you. You have good food to eat. People here love you. You are not as thin as people in the village. I am glad that you are doing well, son."

My father returned to the village before it was dark.

I was able to build a good relationship with the hospital staff. I learned much about the Khmer Rouge—about the purpose of the regime's revolution and its ideals. This knowledge was important to my survival. It was fear that drove them nuts. Most importantly, I learned that they all did have human hearts. They liked to be entertained. They wanted to have a good life. Unfortunately, they did not understand how good their lives were. They killed instead of loved. All they did was follow orders from the Angkar. They did not even know who the Angkar was, if you dared ask them. They would have had so much support from people if there was no killing. For my survival, I mimicked their accent and their expressive attitude. I was amazed that there was never a question of my status as one of the new people. They treated me as if I was one of them.

My condition continued to get worse. The infection spread all over my private parts. I groaned and moaned in pain and kept many others awake at night. The chief of the hospital was very concerned. He put in a request to send me to Paed Srok for intensive treatment. He ordered his staff to bring the buffalo cart to transport me to Paed Srok, also known as Kandiang Hospital. No new people had ever been sent to Paed Srok during that time. Paed Srok was located along Pursat River. Surprisingly, this hospital had modern medications and also had a trained medical doctor. The regime had spared his life so that he could serve them in this old people hospital.

I was treated well at Paed Srok. I received antibiotics and was scheduled for surgery to remove the infected area. My surgery was successful. I stayed in the hospital for about two months after I was completely healed. The nursing staff did not want me to leave. I was their friend; I was their entertainer. The nurses were busy working during the daytime. I only saw them at night, when they would gather so I could tell them stories. There was no television or radio to entertain them; I was it.

I spent my days walking along the river sightseeing. I dared not speak to anyone I saw for safety reasons. Before long, I was homesick. I missed my family. I wondered how they were doing. I told the nurses that I wanted to go back to my village. I had forgotten how hard life was at the village. The nurses told me how hard it would be. They said they could let me visit home and then I could return to the hospital after my visit. I thanked them and told them that I wanted to stay close to my family and that I would not want to return. The staff gave me a pair of shoes and a new outfit as a parting gift. Only the old people had this type of clothing to wear. I packed my extra pair of clothes, and I left the hospital in November 1976.

# CHAPTER 12

# Back to the Village

My home was located at the far end of the village. As I walked along the road in my village, people looked at me strangely. I was unable to recognize anyone, since everyone was bony. I had been away only seven months. The children stood along the road looking at me. They were very skinny and appeared to have only skin covering their bones.

While I was daydreaming, I heard someone call my name. "Moeurn, is it you? Oh my God Buddha, it is you. My son, you have a long, blessed life. You have bones made of gold. I can't believe it. I thought you died in the hospital. Look at you; you are so handsome. Your father will be so happy to see you."

It was my mother. I looked into her beautiful eyes, as I listened to her soft-spoken words. She was kind, and her gentle movement had made her the prettiest woman in the early '40s. However, due to the lack of food and sanitation, she appeared like an eighty-year-old woman. I did not recognize her at first. Her cheekbones popped out of her face, and her large eyes were deep brown. She stepped out of the rice field and slowly walked toward me.

"The last time we heard from you was when your father visited you in the hospital." She held my hand, and I could feel the warmth of her smile. Tears trickled down her wrinkled cheeks; they were tears of joy. "We thought you didn't make it," she continued mumbling.

Her group leader was understanding and appeared happy to see my mother and I reunited. She allowed my mother to take the day off to come home with me. That evening, our family stayed up late. They wanted to know everything that had happened to me while I was away. They still couldn't believe that I was still alive. Everyone in my family was very thin. They received a small daily food allowance for their long hours of work. I thanked God Buddha for He at least kept them healthy.

I was not immediately given any work assignment, since the village chief was not sure whether I had come home to stay or would return to the hospital. So I had free time to roam around the village. While my family was out working in the rice field, I wandered in the village, giving assistance to people who needed help.

I met twin girls who worked in the kitchen union, Chanthou and Kolab. Chanthou is the name of a flower that resembles jasmine, and Kolab is Cambodian for rose. The two of them were the most beautiful young women I had seen in the one and a half years of the Khmer Rouge regime's rule. Both worked as union kitchen helpers. They were in front of the kitchen union, pounding on the rice grains to separate them from their skin. The twins were also new people. I stepped on the grinder to help them pound the rice. We worked and teased one another. We sang old songs, which was prohibited by the Angkar. We shared our past school activities and shared our vision. We seemed to have so much in common. We had a great time. I continued to go back to the kitchen to work with them whenever I could.

# CHAPTER 13

# Life as a Fisherman

After about two to three weeks, the chief of the village finally caught up to my free activities. He said that he appreciated my work around the kitchen but needed me to go out in the field to contribute to the needs of the village. He assigned me to go fishing in the Lake of Tonle Sap with Mr. Thuok and Savuth, who were new people. This work assignment was considered the highest job privilege in our area. My parents were happy with my assignment. Usually, the fishermen would have a few dried fish to bring to their families when they returned home. I would live on the fishing boat and come home once a week to bring fish to the union kitchen. I did not worry about how I would fish, but I was fearful of how I would maneuver the boat, since I did not know how to row. Mr. Thuok and Savuth did not pressure me to learn. They usually did the rowing while I cleaned the fish. They taught me whenever they could. The three of us were in the middle of the water, far away from everything. We were free to do anything as long as the old people did not see or hear us. We continued to bring fish to the village weekly and were able to give some to our families privately.

Mr. Thuok was a great singer. I learned many modern songs from him. Savuth was about a year older than me. He was raised in the capital in an upper-echelon family. He had attended ETAPP (I don't know what the acronym stood for), a private school in which English-speaking educators taught English. Besides Khmer, Savuth spoke French and English fluently. He was extremely intelligent. He was not like the other rich kids I had known from the past. He was down-to-earth. We shared our thoughts and feelings about what was going on in the country. Savuth feared that he might lose his ability to speak foreign languages if he did not practice. He believed that this government would collapse someday. "They are going to need people like us to serve the country, to be able to communicate with foreigners," he insisted. He encouraged me to speak to him in French while he responded in English. With this interaction, I began to familiarize myself with the sounds of English. My ears began to get used to the English, although I did not understand it very much. The three of us made a good team.

The chief of the village disbanded our team during the flood season, when the fish became harder to catch. Mr. Thuok and Savuth were assigned to work in the rice field. I was fortunate to be sent to Pursat River to continue fishing with the old people. At night in the fishing camp, I used my storytelling skills to gain their favor. I realized that storytelling was the only entertainment we had left. I learned how to row the boat against the current. Both my storytelling and my knowledge of how to fish in the river helped me remain in the fishing group for nearly two months. While there, I was treated as a one of the old people.

We returned to the village during harvest season.

# CHAPTER 14

# Dead or Alive

I went back to my harvest group and continued to excel in my harvest skills. I felt like I did not work as hard as others, yet I collected much more rice than they did. At night, under the moonlight, teenagers gathered to sing and dance revolution songs. I joined them nightly to reduce the boredom. We usually were fed well during harvest season.

The joy of summer went by very quickly. The rainy season of 1977 arrived. I was sent back to work in the rice fields. We worked night and day, rain or shine.

All of a sudden, I came down with a deadly, persistent fever. The high fever usually began right before noon and lasted for about an hour. After the fever subsided, I would suffer two to three hours of severe headaches. The first time the fever came, I was in the rice field planting rice. I rolled myself out of the rice field to the levy above the water. Everyone was still in the field working. The armed teenager walked toward me. He used the tip of the cannon to flip me over.

"Is it time to pretend to be sick again, comrade? I knew it. You new people are lazy. We should have killed you all," he said with a laugh.

I was sick, and now I was angry. I was no longer afraid to die. I spoke loudly enough for everyone to hear. "Comrade, I am really sick. You go get the nurse. If she says that I am pretending, you can kill me on the spot."

This Khmer Rouge guard was very upset. He did not expect me to speak to him in a challenging manner. I could see in his eyes how much he wanted to end my life. He called the nurse to come over. "Look at him! Is he really sick?" he demanded.

The nurse put her hand on my forehead and on my body. She nodded her head. "He has a fever."

They sent me back to the planting camp.

Because of the fever, I was not able to go to work for weeks. Since I couldn't go to work, my food allowance was cut in half. Now, besides being ill, I was hungrier than ever. My condition became so severe that I felt death was calling me. I felt I would be better off dead than living through this pain. But I had a strong will to survive.

The leader of the planting group did not want to keep me since I couldn't work. She sent me back to the village. I returned home to live with my parents, Phalla, Pich, Duke, Arun, Aren, and Ravy. Savath, Savan, Samuth, and Samith were on different mobile teams and were still out of town.

Due to my high fever, my hair began to fall out. Before long, I became totally bald. I looked like a ninety-year-old man. I was not able to walk. When I needed to move or to go places, I would ask my little brother to hold me or I just crawled.

My parents left to work early in the morning. Phalla took care of the buffalo with other children. Pich and Duke were about eight and six years old, respectively. They took care of me. Arun and Aren were too little.

Every morning, I would ask my brothers, Pich and Duke, to take me to the woods to look for something to eat. I needed energy to fight the fever that would wrack my body around noon each day. We found seeds, young bamboo, and edible roots. My brothers would give me what they could find, and that little bit seemed to help maintain my energy. When we came back home, my brothers would sit on my back to control my violent chills. We would eat the things we had found after my fever went down in the late afternoon. The fever stayed with me for several weeks, until my father found a healer.

This healer appeared serious about what he was doing. He burned incense and prayed. I couldn't understand a word of his chants. I would let him do anything to me to get rid of the fever.

"Tell me exactly where the chills begin in your body." He turned to my father. "I will burn this virus to cure him."

My father looked at him and at me. It was a silent sign; he was asking me for approval of the burn treatment.

I told the healer the approximate time the fever would come on and pointed to where it started in my body. "It begins in the bottom of my spine. It runs all the way up to my neck. I feel extremely cold. My body's heat is high during and after the shaking," I told him.

The healer prepared three special cotton balls. He had me lay face down, and he placed the cotton balls on my lower back. He placed a small piece of wood in between my teeth. "When you feel the pain, bite on this wood. It will help you to release some pain." He burned the incense and prayed.

He waited until the chilling fever was about to attack before he began the treatment. As soon as I told him that the chilling was about to trigger, he lit the cotton balls. The embers traveled through the cotton and reached my skin. Imagine that you put your finger in a fire and were told not to move and leave it there for a minute or two. It was hot! I grabbed the bamboo poles and bit hard into the wood that the healer had placed between my teeth so that I could endure the pain. My skin burned; it smelled like overcooked meat. I have scars on my back to this day to remind me of how sick I was.

Amazingly, I was cured. I barely survived the disease and starvation that year.

# CHAPTER 15

# The Plow Group

I petitioned the chief of the village to allow me to join the plow group. Though I did not know how to plow, I assured him that I was a fast learner, as he had seen during the planting and harvest seasons. He reluctantly allowed me to join the group. He gave me two oxen for plowing. It took me less than a week to learn how to plow correctly.

I had the fastest oxen, and each had interesting character traits. I named them Lee Siv Long (Bruce Lee) and Chiang Ta Hve. (I named both after Chinese kung fu movie stars.) Bruce Lee liked to push or pick people up with his horns. Cambodian farmers usually wore scarves around their waists. Bruce Lee would approach a farmer from behind, insert his horn between the person's scarf and shirt, pick him up, and then wiggle him off. I was in trouble one time when he picked up my group leader by the scarf and threw him down. The group leader accused me of purposely using my ox to attack him. I was lucky because my peers in the plow group knew about Bruce Lee and explained my ox's behavior to the leader. I couldn't help but chuckle inside. Chiang Ta Hwe loved to kick. His hind legs were dangerous. His side-kicking and back-kicking skills were precise. He even kicked when the big flies bit him.

While neither of the oxen would allow anyone to ride on his back, neither put up any resistance with me. They pulled the plow fast and did not like having anyone in front of them. Because of their speed, they often pushed the plow worker in front of them. I was usually assigned to plow alone in a field to avoid hurting others. It was to my advantage because I could finish my work early and still have time to look for additional sustenance.

In the plow group, we received more food allowance than any other group, but it was still not enough to fill our stomachs. My only concern about staying with the group was that it kept me away from my family. Our work was tedious, and we moved from camp to camp. I was happy with the food allowance but not so happy with the long work hours.

I was very disappointed when the chief of the village switched my oxen for a pair of buffalo. "These buffalo are strong, and they are easy to take care," he told me. "They can eat grass in the water and on the ground. It will be difficult for you to feed your animals at your new assignment because most of the area is under water."

I sadly ran my hands over my oxen's horns and their backs to say good-bye.

Due to my unfamiliarity with buffalo, I had a hard time recognizing mine. To me, all the buffalo were all dark gray with big, long horns. To be sure of which two had been assigned to me, I tied metal plates to their necks. My peers teased me on several occasions, switching the plates and putting them on different buffalo. I would take the buffalo with the plates, which were not mine, to the camp. It took me several weeks before I was able to recognize my buffalo without the metal plates on them.

Once a month, each of the plowman were distributed a pack of cigarettes. Since I did not smoke, I traded them with the smokers for food and other needs. I even managed to trade for a pair of buffalo bells from the nearby village.

Once, someone stole my cigarettes. There were only two other men in my shed, Comrade Khon and Comrade Sreng. Comrade Khon was the one of the old people. He smoked. I assumed that comrade Khon must have taken my cigarettes. I reported him to the group leader. The leader did nothing, since I did not have any evidence.

The next day, the three of us were asked to meet with the plow leader. He looked at me angrily. "Comrade Khon said that he lost his lighter in the shed last night. There were only two of you sharing the shed. Tell me, which one of you took his lighter?"

Both comrade Khon and the leader stared at me. Comrade Sreng and I looked at each other with disbelief. This was the same man whom I had reported to the leader as having possibly taken my cigarettes. Now he accused one of us of stealing his lighter. Comrade Sreng denied taking the lighter.

"Comrade Bong," I tried to defend myself, "I did not take his lighter. I understand the severity of the punishment if I steal. Comrade Sreng has no reason to steal either. I think Comrade Khon is accusing us in retaliation for what I said yesterday. It would be unfair to penalize us for a crime we did not commit." In addition, there was no proof.

I must have made the leader very angry. To him, my response was a form of accusing him of taking sides, which was true. His face turned red. He screamed at me for talking back and for trying to reason with him. He ordered the crew to tie us up.

"One of you will confess to stealing. Tell me now before the situation gets worse," he yelled at us.

Both of my arms were tied back with a piece of rope, right above my elbows. My chest was tight. Comrade Bong and his men forced us to kneel on the ground to interrogate us. They whipped us every time we said no and insisted that we had not stolen the lighter. We fell to the ground. We rolled back and forth to endure the pain. They then tied us to the wheel of the buffalo cart so that we would remain standing. They assumed that I was the one who had stolen the lighter to avenge the loss of my cigarettes, so they let Comrade Sreng go. They continued to whip me, asking me where I had hidden the lighter. Blood filled the whip prints. I continued to deny stealing. The pain of the beating was not as severe as the emotional torture and insults. I was angry. I felt like blood was pouring from my eyes. I resented Comrade Khon's accusation. I do not remember when they stopped whipping me.

I was left on the wheel overnight. As I tried to rest on the wheel while everyone was asleep, I felt a heavy bang on my head. The next morning when I gained consciousness, I found myself next to the wheel, untied. My head hurt. I felt stickiness on my face. I peeled the dried blood from my eyes to look around. My body was covered with marks from the whip and dried blood. I had an enormous headache. I ran my fingers through my hair, finding an open wound. Thorns were imbedded deep into my skull. I crawled back to my shed and removed the thorns one by one. The stick that the person had hit me with must have had thorns growing on it. It had probably come from an Angkrong tree. I dared not ask or try to investigate who had attacked me. I stayed silent and hoped that the worst was over.

# CHAPTER 16

# Near Death Experiences

Another time while I was with the plow group, I found myself in a state between life and death. The sky filled with dark, gray clouds, and rain poured from the sky. First, following my spooked buffalo and then unsure of where I was going, I ran crazily and wandered into a village I didn't know. I stood under an awning and watched the rain sweep savagely across the muddy walkway. My heart pounded with fear. I was quivering. What was wrong here? I wondered. Then it dawned on me. *Amazing, no one is in the village. What is going on?* I asked myself, trembling.

A moment earlier, I had been lying under a tree, listening to the rhythm of the buffalo bells mix with the birds' songs. It had reminded me of what I'd had a few years before—*freedom*. Remembering the smile on the American face during the embassy evacuation, I'd imagined what my life would have been if I had gone to America when that marine had made the offer. I couldn't turn back the clock. I had missed my golden opportunity. All I had now was a grandiose hope that someone would come and rescue me from this miserable life. I refused to die. I had looked at my buffalo and seen that they had a better life than I did. They enjoyed themselves on the green prairie, while I hardly had enough food to eat. I could be beaten or killed at anytime by these Khmer Rouge rulers.

Lying under that tree, I had been plunged into a dream I wouldn't soon forget. I saw myself floating in the sky. I was among white clouds. I was afraid and felt that I was lost. Suddenly, two angels on a flying boat sailed toward me. I asked them for food and the way to get back home. I told them how hard our life was and how little food we had. They grabbed me and put me in the boat. Handing me a bowl of rice, the angels told me to eat it all and I would be saved.

I laughed and told them that I could eat ten times more. Strangely, when I began to eat, the bowl kept filling itself. I must have eaten for a long time. Finally, the angels smiled and said, "You may go back." They pushed me, and I fell off the boat. I experienced in my stomach that feeling that many of us have experienced when, in a dream, we fall from a building or tree or some other great height, only worse. Then I heard, *bang, bang*. It was the sound of thunder.

My dream had broken as the thunder sounded. Lightning had lit up the sky. I'd pulled myself to my feet; it was time to get my buffalo and return to the plow camp. The lightning and thunder were intense, and the lights and sounds had frightened both of my animals. They'd run as fast as they could into the forest. I'd run after them. Unfortunately, I had lost their trail. After searching for a while, I had found myself in this old, empty village hidden in the jungle.

A black blanket of nature rolled in to cover the earth again. It was dark and scary. I stood still, trembling. OR I stood, still trembling. I gazed around, trying to discern a trace of movement in the village. Then the moon came out to replace the sun. I felt hopeless. I would not find my buffalo, and I would be accused of being a traitor; I would be killed if I went back to the plow camp without the buffalo.

The wind blew lightly from the north, bringing strange smells and a frightening noise to my ears. The smell of dead animals' blood surrounded me a lot, filling me with worry. Maybe something bad had happened to my buffalo. I followed the smells in the air. Rain flowed along the trench; the water was dark, possibly red. I kept on going until I found an unimaginable scene.

The unaccounted villagers had been slaughtered and were still on the ground, lying like logs. These people looked like they had been executed only a couple of hours earlier. Some of the bodies were still bleeding. I was in shock. I wanted to move closer to check to see if anyone was still alive. However, my legs seemed stuck in one place, numbed by the horror. I knelt on the ground and prayed for the dead and dying.

"Help, please, someone help me," called a weak voice.

*Someone is still alive!* I said to myself. I walked to where the voice had come from. A young man, about eighteen years old, was soaked with blood. He told me to get out of there quickly and to tell his sister not to come back to the village. The wounded man died before he could tell me who and where his sister was. Then I heard another voice. *There must be many more people still alive.*

I was about to check on others, but I heard people talking from the other side of the bush. "This time we have to make sure that no one is still breathing," a voice said.

I did not have time to run. I rolled myself under a pile of corpses. I could feel the footsteps of the Khmer Rouge coming toward me. My heart pounded with fear. The Khmer Rouge circled and bayoneted the bodies. Some of them were still alive, screaming for mercy. It was so cruel and senseless. I clenched my teeth. I closed my eyes and prayed, waiting for the bayonet to nail my stomach.

*    *    *

I grabbed my head. I hugged myself and searched my body to see if I had been stabbed. I found nothing. *I am still alive!* I assured myself.

I had been unconscious for the whole night. Even though I was still alive, I was not very joyful. I had lost my buffalo. I would be killed if I could not find them. I decided to go back to the camp anyway. I prayed that the greatness of my mother's milk, which had saved my life the night before, would give me a chance and would guide my buffalo home.

My prayer was answered. My buffalo had found their way to the plow camp during the night when the rainstorm ceased.

# CHAPTER 17

# Devastation

Due to a great demand for patient care, each village opened its own hospital. The Angkar continued to use the herbal and traditional medicine to treat people. Only the old people were treated with Western medicines or transferred to the Paed Srok hospital when they were gravely ill.

September 1977 was a bad month for my family, if not the worst. I was told that my mother, my father, and my four little brothers were sick, and they all were in the hospital. My father had fallen out of a tree after being assigned to gather wood for the village kitchen. My brother-in-law had passed away weeks before. A buffalo had rammed him in the chest, and he had never recovered from the injury. During the Khmer Rouge, if you went to the hospital, you would likely never get out. The majority of people who went to the hospital in my town died. The hospital staff would dig one big hole and wait until the end of the day to bury the dead. Six to ten bodies would fill each grave. Death was common in light of the lack of proper care, food, and good medications.

I was allowed to go home for two days to visit my sick family. Duke had already passed away by the time I got there. My mother told me that he'd died of starvation, not disease.

"Duke asked for a piece of rice before he died, but those unkind nurses wouldn't give it to him," my mother said.

"I am going to eat only clean food so I won't die like brother Duke," said Arun.

I put my hand on his head and assured him that he was going to be okay.

Pich and Aren lay on the bamboo bed with sad eyes. They looked at me hopelessly. They seemed too tired to talk; however, I could see in their eyes that they were happy to see me. My mother appeared to be the strongest, compared to me and everyone else. My chest felt tight as I watched the scene in the hospital.

I could feel the warmth of my tears running down my cheek as I looked at my father. I could see his bones, which were covered by his thin, wrinkled skin. His movements were very limited. He had not been able to get up since he'd fallen from the tree. I'd managed to save a pack of cigarettes to give to him. A pack of cigarettes was valued at about an ounce of pure gold during that time. He smiled at me weakly. I knew that, if he could, he would have gotten up to hug me and let me know how much he loved me. He moved his hand slowly and touched mine. I opened my palms and gently massaged his hands and arms.

My mother whispered to me that my father had not just fallen from the tree. "They were upset when your father could not collect enough wood for them. Your father worked hard to please them. He climbed up trees to cut dead branches. He fell and hurt himself. When he got back, they said that your father was lazy and had pretended that he was hurt. So they hit him. We could not complain of his illness, which was due to the additional beating."

She told me the hospital staff would not give them any medication and would not allow them to return home. "The leader said that sick people must be in the hospital. They don't eat like healthy people. Sick people are a burden to the village. They are useless. I may be starved, but I'm not sick. I want to be with him," she added, as she looked at my father, "and your brothers. That is why I pretend that I am sick." My mother said that we needed to keep our mouths shut to stay alive.

My mother would sneak out of the hospital to go fishing and pick up edible leaves or dig for edible roots to add to the food that the hospital distributed to the patients. I spent a day with my mother in the hospital and another day at home with my widowed sister and my younger sister.

Two weeks later, while I was in the plow camp, I was told that my father, Pich, and Arun had died in the hospital. I was shocked to learn that my father and Arun had died within minutes of each other.

My mother was devastated. "I did not know what to do. Your brother appeared as though he suffocated while your father took his last breath. I wanted to die with them, but I still had Pich and Aren with me."

My mother asked to be released from the hospital after Pich died. She went home with my baby brother, Aren.

I requested time off to visit my mother and to pay respects to my father and brothers.

"Can you bring your father back from the grave?" my leader asked me. "You just had time off a couple of weeks ago. I cannot allow you to go again."

In my anguish, I heard myself laughing as I walked away. It was a laugh I could never forget.

*     *     *

"Honey, wake up! Are you okay? Would you like some water?"

I glanced quickly at my wife, who had just awoken me. I heard a buzz in my ear. Yes, I was still on the plane ride. I tried to catch my breath, as I responded to her, "Yes, a cup of water, please."

I went back to sleep after drinking the water.

# CHAPTER 18

# Unforgettable

The plow season was over. I was sent home in late November 1977. Aren was still very sick. I thanked God that my mother, Samith, Samuth, Phalla, Savath, and Savan were healthy. But they were bony. My little niece, Ravy, was in the girls' group. She was also healthy. This was good news.

Food in the village was still scarce. New people still needed to go out to look for other means to supplement their diet. I was assigned to take care of a herd of buffalo and cow with Samuth. One of the old people, Comrade Eam, was assigned as our shepherd leader. The job was strenuous and tedious. I had been strong when I'd first returned to the village, but my energy level began to deteriorate as the days went by. My high fever was back, though I still went to work to reserve the right to receive a full food allowance.

One day before I left for work, my mother asked me to leave half of my food allowance for Aren. She told me that she had already given him half of hers.

"He may not survive without some more food. He is very weak," she added.

I looked at my brother, who was lying on the rags. I'd seen no movement in his eyes or his body. He appeared to barely cling to life. I did not know if my share of rice would keep him alive, but I knew for sure that I needed this little bit of rice for energy to get myself to work.

"Mother, I have to go to work. I need this food for strength. I am sick too, you know," I replied. Then I left for work.

When I returned from work on that same day, I found my mother sitting in the corner inside the house. She looked at me and at the dirty rags that covered Aren. He had died that morning. I sat down silently. I felt that if she and I could shed any tears, our tears would be a river. My head hung between my knees; I grabbed it with both hands. I looked down, and many thoughts ran through my head. I felt remorseful for not doing enough to save my brother's life.

Finally, my mother spoke to me. "Moeurn, if you would have just given your brother that half of your food, he would probably still be alive now, wouldn't he?"

I continued to sit silently, confused. I wondered what could have made me so selfish, so blind, so filled with mean spirits. Was it deprivation? Yes, I would have probably saved my brother's life with half of my allowance, and yes, I would have still lived that day. My guilt and sorrow would grow as time passed.

I told my mother I would bury Aren the next day. I lay next to Aren's body, exhausted, and fell asleep. The next morning, Samuth and I wrapped Aren's body and carried it to the back of our home. The bamboo bushes were no more than two hundred yards from our home. The ground was hard and tough. We were weary with fatigue. We were only able to dig down as deep as our knees. I gently placed my brother on his back in the hole. We cut Angkrong's tree with its thorny branches to put between the dirt and the body to keep the wolves away. We knelt to pay our respects, and then left.

\*    \*    \*

Hunger was everywhere among the new people. People committed heinous crimes just for food. They would eat anything to survive. I had to watch my buffalo herd closely. A couple of my buffalo had already lost their tails. Someone had cut them off for food while I was not watching. In the graveyard, new burial sites were dug up, and parts of the bodies, such as the buns and breasts, were cut out. Some of these cannibals went as far as to kill people for food.

I heard some horror stories from the old people. A man pretended to ask for a cigarette lighter. When he was given the lighter, his companion would jump out of the bush and kill the owner of the lighter from behind. Most of the victims of this type of crime were old people. For the most part, they were the ones who owned the lighters and were healthier. Perhaps these killings might be termed crimes of passion or revenge, or perhaps they constituted a new category of crime that I had not before been known to me—simply crimes of "food deprivation." It led me to believe that human behavior is not much different from that of animals when starvation abounds.

I remember two boys who were about ten and twelve years old. They lived with their ailing mother in the back of our hut. We heard them cry almost daily, asking for food. For two days, we did not hear them cry for food. Out of curiosity, we went to check on them. We found them hiding in the mosquito net. The boys had their mother's head in the pot. They had made a soup of her. I just hope that their mother was dead before she was decapitated and made into a pot of soup. The village leader was angry. He took the boys to the woods, about one hundred yards from the home, and one by one, he chopped them into pieces.

One day, a buffalo was stuck in the mud. Samuth and I were not able to pull it out; the more we pulled, the deeper it sank.

The leader threw me a big ax. "Tonight, we will have buffalo meat for dinner."

I was happy with the meat offering but deadly scared of what was going to happen next. He expected me to kill the buffalo. I had never killed a buffalo before. I was afraid to say no to my leader. But I did not know how I could do it. I could barely pick up the heavy ax, let alone swing it at the buffalo.

Now, it was me against the buffalo. We looked into each other's eyes, both full of fear. I had once been told that we could kill a cow or buffalo by striking it in between the horns. I gathered my energy, picked up the ax, and swung as hard as I could at the buffalo's head with my eyes closed. When I opened my eyes, I saw the buffalo still looking at me. Out of fear, I kept swinging at the buffalo's head. My leader counted the blows I made. He lost count after forty.

# CHAPTER 19

# The Cornfield

The harvest season of 1978 was over quickly. The Angkar planned to clear the jungle to plant corn. They formed a big group composed of single males and females. They divided the big group into five different small groups. Each small group contained thirty to thirty-five members. The five groups were under the supervision of two armed Khmer Rouge guards. Because of my hard-working habits and good behavior, I was selected to be one of the small group leaders. Usually, leaders were chosen from among the old people.

Each night, we conducted group meetings to criticize one another for improvement. The Khmer Rouge called these meetings "Constructive Support Group." I told my group that I would rather die of overwork than be executed because of laziness or tardiness. I told them that, if we worked hard, something good would happen to us. Within a matter of weeks, my group was able to clear a much larger area in the jungle than the others. We were recognized by the Angkar for our hard work. My team was the leading squad in the field. This meant that we received a better food allowance. I continued to lead my workers in the field. I worked as hard as my group members, if not harder. I did not sit and order them to clear the jungle. I led them in the field. My group trusted me.

The Angkar recognized that our group had bonded, and it scared them. The chief of the village came to observe the progress. The armed guards had reported to her our team's achievement.

The chief of the village broke my team up. She transferred me to supervise those in the detention camp, the wrongdoers. The Angkar also called these people inmates. The detainees were confined due to tardiness and laziness. They were weak and did not meet the expectations of the Angkar. One of the inmates was my brother,

Phalla. To me, I felt that it was a test of my commitment and my ability to be impartial. If I ever favored my brother in any way, I, as well as my brother, would be killed instantly.

As a team leader, I received a much larger food allowance than did the rest of the group. The chef also made special food for me every meal. I usually grabbed a couple of bites and walked away. The group would take my leftovers and share them among themselves. I did this because I did not want the Angkar to think that I played favorites, especially when my little brother was an inmate here. We could be killed if they suspected that I gave food to my brother. I would get my extra food from the kitchen when I returned to the camp.

In the Khmer Rouge regime, if you had sex outside of marriage, you had gone against the Angkar morals, and you would be subject to execution. Boys and girls were afraid to speak to one another for fear they would be thought to be in love. As new people, we did not care about love. We had no desire for intimacy. All we were thinking about was food and living for one more day.

Abraham Maslow's five hierarchies of need applied well to this situation. The bottom rung included physical needs, such as food, air, and shelter. The next four—security, love and belonging, self-esteem, and self-actualization—were not then priorities. We, at least I, did not think of those, much less desire to achieve them, when our basic needs, such as food and shelter, were not met. The Khmer Rouge deprived us, and they made sure that we could never achieve the next level of needs. The tactic of keeping the new people struggling to fulfill their first level of needs worked well for the Khmer Rouge. They were able to stay in full control of us. We could never achieve the next stage—security or love and belonging.

A few months into the corn season, one of our female workers was raped and killed. The Angkar sent investigators, along with the second in command from the village, Comrade Bo. Comrade Bo was married and had a couple of children. With curly hair and light skin, he was a handsome man compared to all the other old people. He looked like a gentleman. He was soft-spoken and appeared much smarter than many old people; he could read and write very well. When he talked, people listened. He attracted and was attracted to the old people, who found him to be powerful and lovable.

But he was deadly in his decision making. New people were not fooled by his handsome looks. Everyone in the field was very scared. Khmer Rouge investigators did not need evidence to catch and kill. The suspects were questioned and, of course, killed. If the suspects named anyone involved, the Khmer Rouge would fetch that person and kill him or her as well. The Khmer Rouge would ask the suspect, under duress and torture, who else was involved in the crime. Then the guards would kill the suspect after the interrogation was done.

Two of the group leaders were accused and executed. The executioners bound the feet of one of the leaders and dragged him behind a horse until he died.

One of the group leaders asked me and the other leaders to have a meeting regarding the execution. Each of us denied any involvement in the rape case. We did not know whether the two leaders who were killed had actually been involved in the rape and murder. We feared that maybe someone did not like them and had taken this opportunity for revenge; the trend of catching and killing suspects would have made such a scenario more than probable. We anticipated that they would arrest one of us soon. All three of us joined hands and promised that, if one of us were accused and arrested, the accused would accept his fate and keep his mouth shut in order to break the killing chain.

One of the leaders shouted, "I will not forgive anyone, not even you guys, if I am accused of this. My soul will come back to haunt you and take you away."

Sadly, that leader was arrested the next day. The guards tied his hands and had him pulled behind a horse to the village for questioning. He was then eliminated. The case was closed after that. I guess he kept his promise to break the chain of killing, and the plan did work. We were safe for the moment.

Due to the instability at the cornfield, Comrade Bo was assigned to supervise the cornfield until the season was over. Along with Comrade Bo, there was a nurse, Comrade Leap. For one of the old people, she was beautiful. She had long, shiny hair with dark, smooth skin, and her face was decorated by a pair of beautiful, sharp eyes. She was one of the old people who we respected. She listened, and she cared. Unfortunately, she fell for Comrade Bo's charms. They became romantically involved. Many of us knew of their involvement, but we did our part by pretending not to know, or we might be killed. In the Khmer Rouge regime, only husband and wife were allowed to sleep together. There was no such thing as a lover or a boyfriend or girlfriend. You would be killed instantly if those in charge found out that you were having sex.

Before long, Comrade Leap became pregnant. The chief of the village found out and ordered the armed guards, who had meals with both Comrade Bo and Comrade Leap daily, to kill them for breaking the morality rule. For me, it was incomprehensible to see these four people, who ate and laughed together daily, come to this. Both armed guards had known about the involvement and had done nothing until they were ordered to kill their friends. How could they do it?

The corn season ended, and the rainy season started. The Angkar called a meeting with the group leaders to make plans to close the cornfield operation. The two guards wanted me to give them input regarding the detainees I supervised. I had to be very careful of what I said. The wrong words could jeopardize my life. Instead, I questioned them about their plans. They told me that these people were criminals—they would influence the good society when they returned to the village. The Angkar wanted to have them killed.

I said to myself, *That is disgusting.* My brother Phalla had come to work late, served his time for three months in the strictest environment with little food allowance, and now these people had labeled him as criminal and wanted to kill him. I could not let this happen. I tried to control my emotions; I could not allow them to know how concerned I was. I laughed and nodded my head, in agreement. Then I spoke up, "However, these criminals could be very useful to the Angkar if we kept them alive. I do not think that they would likely repeat the same offense again if we split them up. We should send them back to the village to work in the rice fields. But, of course, the decision is yours, comrades."

Both of the guards stared at me, perhaps surprised because I had offered an idea. They told me that they would let me know after they consulted with the chief of the village.

The good news was that all inmates were released when the camp closed.

# CHAPTER 20

# The Wedding

One day, the Khmer Rouge invited all the single young men and women to a social meeting. The Angkar prepared for us a special feast. After the meal, the chief of the village announced that we were at the brink of having plenty of food to eat and were able to self-govern without the help of foreigners. What we needed was to increase our population. Now it was the time for us to start families.

Then, the chief of the village, who was also a beautiful, single woman, began to pair up men and women. She performed eight marriages that day.

That evening, she called me to meet her at the headquarters. I was terribly frightened. I thought I must have done something wrong. She must have called me to tell me what I had done and then she would kill me. I went home to my mother. I told her about the meeting tonight and asked what I should do.

My mother cried. She told me that no new people in the village knew what the chief looked like. She'd heard that if anyone looked the chief in the eye, she would kill the person. She had killed many villagers, either by her own hand or by ordering her armed guards to kill. My mother suggested that I should run. I reminded her that I practically had no place to run and that, if I were to run, I would jeopardize the family's lives. I'd had a good rapport with the chief in the past and hoped that would work in my favor. I decided to take a chance; I would meet with her, and I was prepared to accept my fate.

The village chief had her staff prepare dinner for us. She dismissed them after the dinner was set on the floor mat. She invited me to take the first bite, which was quite unusual and an honor. Then we ate silently. I was confused. My heartbeat was out of rhythm. There were multiple courses on the plate, but I did not enjoy them very much. I felt as if I were swallowing a rock with every bite I took. I was anxious to hear what she had to say.

After the dessert, she looked at me with her beautiful but sad eyes. "The event that happened today will have an effect on everyone in the village and the district."

My heart pounded as I listened to her soft voice. *After all, she is human*, I thought. She had showed passion and some fear about her uncertain future. She appeared to realize that she must do everything—I mean everything—that the Angkar asked her to do. I put my head down after I took a quick look at her face.

Then she continued. "The Angkar ordered me to perform as many weddings as I could to pair the young people up. I know that I am no exception to the order of the Angkar. The Angkar will pair me up and marry me to someone who I have never known before, just like I did to the others today." She stopped and took a deep breath before she went on. "As you might know, the Angkar wanted to pair old people with old people and new people with new people. There is only one exception. A man of the old people will have a choice of marrying someone who is old or new."

I began to understand why I was here. I had a sense of where the speech would end. I had goose bumps as I gave her a dry smile and continued to listen.

"Comrade Moeurn, I wish you were old people. I would have . . ." She stopped, and her face turned peachy.

I nodded my head as a sign of my understanding, but I was still amazed at the situation I was in. I recalled the time when I was in the cornfield working. She would often ask her escort to invite me back to the village to have dinner with her. At the time, I had thought it was because I had done a good job on the cornfield and part of her routine to keep apprised of the progress of our work in the field. I was so naive and innocent. My only goal was to survive this deadly time, and thus, I would do whatever I was asked to do to avoid being killed. I turned my attention back to the present when she continued.

"Comrade Moeurn, I do like you a lot. Therefore, I am going to give you a chance to pick your own mate. I will wed you with the woman of your choice. You do not have much time."

I was afraid to say anything. I thanked her for her compassion and companionship and for the opportunity.

Before I left, she told me that she had arranged with the chief of economy in the village to have me drive the buffalo cart. I would travel to Khet, the city province, to pick up food and supplies with other drivers. This was one of the most prestigious jobs in the village. I was very happy about the new assignment.

I went home to my mother to tell her the good news. My mother was happy to see me alive and to learn that I had received such a great job in the village. With this job, I would have extra rice and dried fish to eat and could send some of it to my family. I told my mother that one of my concerns was finding someone to marry. I told her that I did not feel that I was ready for love. Getting married was the last thing on my mind at that time. I asked my mother if she had heard anything from the twins, Kolab and Chanthou. They had both seemed to get along well with me, and I would not mind marrying one of them. My mother said that they had both been sent to the mobile group two years earlier and no one had heard from them.

"You are the luckiest young man in the village. Any girl would be a fool if she refused your proposal. You are blessed by the powers that be. Go out and look for my daughter-in-law," she finished with a smile.

While no one knew what I was doing, I went around the village mobile teams to speak with many young girls. I tried to find one that I might like and hoped that I would see Kolab or Chanthou.

A week passed by, and I still had not found anyone I liked. The village chief was anxious. She began to pressure me. I went to the other mobile team that had just returned from their out of town assignment. I heard that Chanthou was among the group. I was so excited that I would finally meet her again. But Chanthou is a common female name in Cambodia, and the girl was another Chanthou; I should have known. This Chanthou had lighter skin than most girls in the group. She was smaller in stature than my other Chanthou. Although there was some mud on her face, she still looked very pretty.

She was shy as I approached her. At first, she did not appear to want to speak to me. I didn't know if she knew what I was doing.

Chanthou was different than any girl I had met before. She seemed cautious of what she said and seemed aware of the situation around her. Listening to her speech, I could tell that she was very intelligent. I decided to ask her to marry me. I went to the village chief to inform her and to ask her for rice and dried fishes to give to Chanthou's mother so that I could properly engage myself to her daughter.

That evening, I brought the rice and dried fish to Chanthou's home. Her mother was so happy that her daughter would marry the buffalo cart driver.

"You are a very handsome man. My girl is very lucky to have you. I will let her know when she comes home."

Within a matter of weeks, we grew to love each other. We scheduled the wedding a couple of times, but due to the absence of the village chief, we never got married. During that time, the chief was called to the district frequently for meetings.

# CHAPTER 21

# The New War

We heard a rumor that the Vietnamese were fighting with the Khmer Rouge, and the good news was that the Khmer Rouge had been losing every battle. The district chief called my village chief to meet with him at the headquarters. He arranged for my village chief to marry an older village chief, who was not very attractive. This male village chief had lost one eye in the previous war.

After the arranged marriage had taken place, the district chief sent the couple back to the village with a deadly assignment. They began to execute anyone who talked about the fighting between the Khmer Rouge and the Vietnamese. They told us that it was just a rumor and there were no Vietnamese soldiers in Cambodia. They investigated everyone in the village and killed anyone they suspected of belonging to the Vietnamese network. They also killed anyone who spoke Vietnamese or was of Vietnamese origin. Both of my parents spoke Vietnamese. My father had been a French soldier and fought in the Vietnam War for years. He returned to Cambodia after our country gained independence from France. My mother had a Cambodian Vietnamese friend in the village, and they sometimes spoke Vietnamese to each other. All the group leaders and section leaders knew that she spoke Vietnamese. The Angkar executed my mother's friend, and our family was next in line.

Fortunately, I went home the day that they wanted to take my mother. My mother was crying hysterically.

"They took Comrade Mon's wife," she told me. "They killed her because she speaks Vietnamese. I am the only one who communicated with her in Vietnamese. The Angkar said that, because I speak Vietnamese, I am of Vietnamese descent. I was told that I would be killed." She sobbed as she talked.

I was upset; I knew that we were certainly not of Vietnamese descent. I knew my family's tree very well. Of course, the Angkar could use my mother's ability to speak Vietnamese as a reason to kill us, especially my family; they were not happy with me, as I had a good job with the village chief.

I went to the village chief for help. The chief came to my part of the village and scolded the section leaders.

"Who said that comrade Moeurn and his family are Vietnamese?" she demanded.

No one dared look at her face. She halted the execution. She assured me that, as long as she was around, she would not let that happen to my family. My mother was thankful.

In late 1978, while I was assigned to bring goods to the mountain, I saw many people on the train, going west. I was told that the Angkar were moving them from the far eastern part of the country to our area and Battambang Province to help plant rice.

The fact was that the Khmer were fighting in the east with the Vietnamese. They were moving people out of the war zone. When these people reached their destination, they would be under the close eye of the Khmer Rouge. Anyone who talked about the fighting would be killed instantly. As an old Khmer saying goes, "You cannot cover a dead elephant with a basket."

That's what it was like. Systematically, the guards executed all of the relocated people for not being able to keep their silence. Later, I found that my grandmother, my aunt, my uncle, and my cousins were among the victims of this killing spree. The Khmer Rouge accused the eastern Cambodians of supporting the invasion of Communist Vietnamese.

On at least two occasions, the Angkar had me transport ammo to the frontline. I never told anyone for fear of my life. We moved many villagers to the mountain, Som San, to clear the forest for farming. I was often asked by others and my family about the activities, but I kept silent to protect their lives and mine.

# CHAPTER 22

# Som San Mountain

In the jungle of Som San, Angkar made people work day and night. The mobile teams burned the jungle at night to make way for growing corn and potatoes. One evening, while I was having dinner next to my cart, a young female came to talk to me.

"Comrade Moeurn, my team leader wants to speak with you."

I looked at her. "Who is your leader? Do you know why she wants to speak with me?"

The girl shook her head and led me to her section. As I walked behind her, I wondered, *What did I do now? Did I piss someone off? Am I in trouble?*

Then she pointed to the big tree. "She is waiting for you over there. I will be here." She guarded the area to make sure that I was safe talking to her leader.

I was both nervous and scared at the same time. I walked slowly to the tree. A woman stood there, leaning against the tree on the other side. She commanded me to stop before I came any closer.

"I do not know if you still take care of the flowers you like so much," she said.

*Oh, my Buddha God, I must be in the twilight zone. This woman speaks like we are in a movie scene,* I thought to myself. "What? I don't understand. What do you mean?" I asked.

She continued, "The old Khmer saying says, 'Out of sight, out of mind.' Do you remember that?"

"Of course I know that, but it does not have anything to do with me. Who are you?" I questioned. I could hear her take a deep breath as she walked out of the shadow and into the light of the burning logs. I could see a tear running down her cheek. She gave me a quick look and then turned away.

"Kolab, oh Lord it is you! Where have you been? I was looking all over for you and your sister," I said with joy.

"You were?" she questioned, with a little smile on her face and then continued, "My sister and my parents died about a year ago. I was sent all over the region to work with the mobile team. Do you remember what you told me when we worked together at the village kitchen? What you said has kept me alive. You told me to stay alive and do everything I was asked so I could live. Now I am here. I am alive. My dream was to meet you someday and to possibly build a family together. Every time I see someone from the village, I ask for you. I wanted to know how you were doing and where you were. But no one seemed to know." She stopped, took a deep breath, and continued, "A few weeks ago, I heard that you came up to the mountain often to bring us supplies. I was happy, and I thought that we were destined to be together. My hope melted when I heard that you were engaged." Her tears rained down her cheeks as she stopped talking.

"Kolab, as I said earlier, I was looking for you and your family. I asked my mother and the people in the village. No one seemed to know where you were. I was pressured by the chief to get married. She would have arranged for me to marry someone who I totally did not like if I could not find a girl within a certain period. I am so sorry. I can understand how you feel." I ran out of breath. I took a deeper breath and continued, "For us, it is too late in this life. We need to move on. You know that once engaged, I can't take my word back and run to you. We would both be killed for betraying the Angkar's moral code. We need to continue to live. Where there is darkness, there would be light. I do not believe this is the end of the rope for any of us."

We sat next to each other and continued to talk until the workers went to sleep. We felt much better after seeing each other and being able to express our hidden feelings. We pledged to be friends forever. I would never see Kolab again after I left the mountain.

# CHAPTER 23

# The Separation

Once in a while, we could hear the gunfights between the Khmer Rouge and the Vietnamese soldiers. We just looked at each other and pretended that we were deaf. One evening, while I was sleeping under my buffalo cart, Savuth crawled in and woke me up.

"Comrade Moeurn, the Vietnamese soldiers are nearby. I heard that the Khmer Rouge defense line is broken. I was told that many of us have already escaped to the other side. Your brother, Samith, was in the region where the Vietnamese took over. I think he is already free. My fiancée and I are ready to go. Your fiancée, Chanthou, asked me to come and get you. She is packed. Let's go." He spoke in a rushed tone.

I was excited to hear the news. I told him that I would meet the group after I spoke with my sister, Savath.

"Are you sure you want to leave?" my sister asked. "You do not know for sure that you will survive the escape. But one thing we know for sure is that, after you leave, we will all be killed. The chief trusts you and believes in you. If you leave, she will kill us all in retaliation." My sister was right. "Do you remember when we were accused of being Vietnamese? Without her defending us, we would have been killed. Think about it. You can do whatever you want to do, but remember the consequences that will follow your decision."

She made sense. I could not just leave and have my family killed. If we were to escape, we must all escape together. But at that time, my mother was in the village. Savan, Samuth, Phalla, and Ravy were in a separate camp, too far to reach. I decided to stay with my sister. The group left without me.

I woke up the next morning, looking for Chanthou. She had left with the group without saying good-bye. I was hurt and missed her terribly. My tears ran down my cheeks as I prepared my buffalo cart to move on. Many of my friends, male and female, tried to comfort me, but it did not seem to help. I came up with many "what ifs" in my head and continued to cry.

The group escaped successfully. Later, my brother Samith, who was already free on the other side, told me that Chanthou waited for me for several months before her aunt forced her to marry another man. She fought with her aunt, refusing to marry. Finally, she gave up because she did not have any means of support. She told Samith that she still loved me.

# CHAPTER 24

# The Great Escape

The Vietnamese Communists invaded Cambodia in January 1979. They took control of most of the highways and cities in Cambodia. People living in the remote areas, like my family, did not know of these events. Whoever had the knowledge of the Vietnamese invasion and talked about it was put to death. The Khmer Rouge moved us from place to place. They took us to Som San Mountain. Many of us died due to the scarcity of water, disease, and poor sanitation.

I thought I would meet Kolab at Som San, but instead I was sent back to the cornfields with an armed Khmer Rouge and two fourteen-year-old boys, Comrade Sah and Comrade Khuon. Comrade Sah was a Khmer Muslim. He was tall and thin by nature, not from starvation. He was from Koh Thom, Kandal Province. Although he was not a fisherman, his family had a long history in the fishery industry. It did not take long to teach him how to fish. His brother, Saleh, had been in a plow group with me. Saleh and I had been close, and we had taken care of one another. I had not seen Saleh since the Angkar had split up the plow group. I was told that he had died. I did not want to ask how he'd died. I was afraid knowing the circumstances would upset me more.

Comrade Khuon was a native. Although he was not one of the old people, he had been born and raised here, in the region. all of his family were from Pursat. Therefore, farming, fishing, and taking care of buffalo were not new to him. He was fast, strong, and very helpful.

The three of us worked well together. Our tasks were not so difficult for us. So, we sent fish to the village a couple times a week as scheduled. The section leader provided us a pair of buffalo and a buffalo cart for transportation. The leader also assigned an armed guard to supervise us. The guard's wife and children remained back at the village. This man was transferred from another region to our village. We did not know his name. We called him Mitt Bong, which means comrade Bong. *Bong* is a Khmer word that we used to address a person who is slightly older, or sometimes much older, depending on the relationship between the persons. Mitt Bong had the authority to kill us at any time.

I was very familiar with the cornfields. After all, I was one of the people who had cleared this jungle to grow corn the previous season. We began to work the soil and plant seeds. It was a blessed season for us. Our watermelons bore hundreds of fruit. The beans grew nicely, and there were many fish to catch. Since there was not much rice sent from the village, Khuon, Sah, and I ate watermelons with fish for breakfast, lunch, and dinner. We must have done this for a month. Mitt Bong had his own rice that he would not share with us. I would stop eating watermelons after the Khmer Rouge regime. I guess I had eaten too many of them.

The rain came down very hard one night. It put out the fire I had built to keep the mosquitoes away from my buffalo. The mosquitoes attacked my buffalo when the rain stopped. They broke their ropes and ran. I did not know the animals were gone until the next morning. While I went out to look for them, Mitt Bong reported the loss to the chief of the village. I looked for them all day, but I couldn't find them anywhere. Two days later, I received a note from my trusted friend that the section leader had ordered my execution. He accused me of releasing the buffalo to the Vietnamese, and as traitor, I would be killed. I was told that the chief of the village who had often rescued me before was out in the battlefield, so I could not count on her to help. Mitt Bong had not heard the order from the section leader yet.

I had made up my mind long before; I would not allow them to kill me. I made my plan of escape. That afternoon, I had a talk with Mitt Bong.

"Mitt Bong, when was the last time you saw your family?" I asked.

"Well, a couple months ago; why?" he responded.

"I think you should go visit them tonight," I said, expressing my sincere concern. "We have lots of dried fish and watermelons. You could take some to your family."

"Tonight? No way, I can't. The chief would punish me if she knew that I left you guys alone here."

"Who would tell her, Mitt Bong? You? I won't. As a matter of fact, I heard that she is out of town. Only the section leaders are in charge in the village. They dare not challenge you. Ha, I will get you some good dried fish. You can take them to your family. All you have to do is come back before the sun rises. I am sure that no one would know you left."

Mitt Bong looked at me and showed some kind of satisfaction and trust. I reassured him that no one would bother us while he was away. I told him that my gesture was just to say thanks for his protecting the three of us.

"You are right. I have not seen my family for quite some time. I also need to discuss the missing buffalo with the section leader. We do need a replacement for transportation of the goods back to the village," said Mitt Bong.

I was very happy that he agreed to leave and even happier to know that he still did not know that he had been ordered to execute me.

As soon as he departed, I packed up my belongings and prepared to escape my impending death. Khuon and Sah begged to come along. I told them it would be dangerous. They did not have an execution to face. It was better for them to stay. They did not take no for an answer. They told me that all their relatives were dead. They had nothing left to live for. They felt that they had a better chance of survival through escape than to wait for the Vietnamese to rescue them. They said that I was like a brother to them. They touched my heart. The last time I had run away was about three years ago, with my two brothers. It seemed as if the scene was to repeat itself. I finally agreed to let them come along.

I had them help me prepare food and all the necessary equipment for the trip. We took our three-by-twelve-foot sailboat to escape. My goal was to cross the great lake of Tonle Sap. The crossing distance was a little over thirty kilometers. I had a feeling that the Vietnamese soldiers probably occupied the other side of the lake. The shore on the other side was closer to the highway than ours. We anticipated that we might face the Khmer Rouge during the journey, so we packed with us spears, a sword, and a nail slingshot for defense. We knew we could use them very well as weapons. Per my calculation, our food would last us for a week. We could not leave until about three in the morning.

We rowed the boat quietly along the riverbank that led to the great lake and arrived at the lake at dawn. Suddenly, there were gunshots, and bullets flew directly at us. The gunshots sounded like corn popping. Now we knew that there were many of them on the shore. They either fought against the Vietnamese or shot at us. From what I saw, the bullets flew directly at us.

The last thing we did to protect ourselves was to put the paddles down and pray. You might find it funny, but it worked. We prayed to the Gods we knew or had heard people talk about, including Jehovah, Jesus, Allah, and the island's leprechauns. We asked them to provide us with spiritual shield and wind to push our boat off the shore. Our prayers were answered. The wind began to blow. I quickly raised the sail, and the boat took off like a bird. We sailed till midday and rested when the wind vanished. We dropped the anchor and cooked lunch. Then we rested for an extra hour before we continued our journey.

We had no idea where we were. All I knew was that, if I went northeast, I would either reach the other side of the lake or go all the way to the capital, Phnom Penh. I made sure to keep my boat in that direction.

In the late afternoon, we saw a small island and a big boat—about fifty times larger than our own. Smoke rose from the island. It appeared that whoever was there was cooking food. Then I saw at least ten people jump off the big boat and walk toward us. They carried knives and sticks. We felt butterflies in our stomachs. I told Sah to aim the slingshot at them. I asked Khuon to get ready in case they became aggressive. Khuon held his spear, ready for action. I had the sword in my hand. I commanded those people to stop walking toward us. I warned them that we would shoot them if they did not stop. They stood still.

The man who was probably the leader of the group shouted at us. "We are not bad people. We ran away from the Khmer Rouge. I think you did too. We need your help with directions."

"Please help us," someone yelled from the boat.

*They are either very smart because they can tell who we are or very dumb for putting everyone's life in danger*, I said to myself. *What if I was the Khmer Rouge? They all would be killed.*

I studied their environment. Little children ran on the island. Some were crying. My gut feeling told me that, yes, they must be running away from the Communists as well.

I asked the man who had spoken on behalf of the group to come closer with his hands up so I could see his face. It was easy to distinguish between the Khmer Rouge and the new people by just looking into people's faces. Most Khmer Rouge and the old people had darker skin, and their dialect was very different. I was assured that he could not harm us, given that he was in the deep water and we were in the boat with all the weapons. The man walked closer to us. I now could tell that he was not one of them. We agreed to come ashore. They all came to us, telling us that they were lost and their food would not last for long. I felt very bad for them, but we could not share our food with close to one hundred people either. I asked them to gather all the clothes that they could cut open. I helped them use these clothes to make a sail and taught them how to use it. I told them how they could tell the direction by looking at the stars at night. I said that I did not know where we could get rescued, but if they kept themselves a distance from the shore and sailed along the lake in a northeasterly direction, they would either reach the opposite shore of the lake or the capital city. I told them that we had to leave, and if we were rescued before them, we would let others know about them.

We sailed until it was dark before we stopped for dinner. After dinner, we continued our trip. "We must not waste time. We need to keep going," I told the boys.

After a few hours of sailing, we heard gunshots again. We thought that, probably, the Khmer Rouge and Vietnamese were fighting each other. Before we knew it, bullets and small rockets flew in our direction, like fireworks. It was time again to go with the wind. I pointed my boat to the north, where the alligator stars headed up. The boat rushed smoothly away from the danger.

Just before we celebrated and thanked the wind, all the stars disappeared. I knew that we should expect the worst—a rainstorm was coming. I put down my sail immediately, as I felt the strong wind from the south. The waves increased in size, and the rain poured down with the strong wind. I could not navigate the boat. All we could do was to try to empty water from the boat. The rainstorm lasted about two hours. We were so exhausted that we fell asleep without anchoring the boat.

We woke to the sun shining brightly in our eyes. We found ourselves ashore on the other side of the lake. I was worried. I had no idea what kind of people we would meet. We pulled the boat away from the shore, just enough so that we would feel safe. We met a group of fishermen. I told Khuon and Sah to be ready, since we did not know what kind of people they were. I asked them to leave the talking to me. Something—I'm not sure what—inspired me to come up with a test to see if people we met were safe.

"Brothers, would you please help us?" I asked. "There was a bad storm last night. We were pushed by the wind and could not find our way home. Could you tell us how to get back?" I did not use the word *comrade*, which is the Khmer Rouge's language. Instead, I used *brothers*; we used this form of address more generally.

"Brother, where are you from?" one of the fishermen responded.

"We are from Pursat, Phum Thmey. We are lost. Where are we?" I was more comfortable now that he'd called me brother instead of comrade.

The man chuckled before he answered. "You are in the Kampong Thom Province, on the other side of the lake. I've never heard of your village. Honestly, I don't know how to tell you to get back home. If you are willing to leave your boat here, you can go by truck along the highway. The Vietnamese soldiers' trucks are up and down the highway. They can give you a ride for free if you don't have the money."

My body shivered, and warm tears ran down my cheeks. I cried with joy. *I'm rescued*, I told myself. I smiled at the boys to let them know that we were safe. Then I told the fishermen the truth. I apologized for being cautious and explained why I had not told them the truth at first. They understood. I asked them to watch for a big boat that was behind us.

We stayed in the water and helped the fishermen fish all day. It was difficult to understand their dialect at first, but we grasped it as time went by. When night fell, we went home with them. We arrived in their village on the evening of April 17, 1979, exactly four years from the day the Communists had taken over the capital. April 17 was also a couple days after the Cambodian New Year celebration.

This was the first year that Cambodians were able to celebrate the New Year since the Communist takeover on April 17, 1975.

We danced to the beat of homemade drums under the moonlight. The villagers greeted us and hosted us, offering us delicious food—chicken soup with fresh weed leaves. It was one of the best evenings I'd had in four years.

Many villagers wanted us to stay with them and promised to take good care of us. Some even offered me their daughter's hand in marriage. Soon after 1979, the ratio of men to women was one to four, and it was still higher in some areas. Finding a man to marry your young daughter off to was very rare.

My primary goal was to find my family. Starting my own family was the last thing on my mind. I thanked the villagers for their hospitality and the offers. I told them that I needed to find my family first.

# CHAPTER 25

# In Search of Family

I said good-bye to the family with whom I'd stayed overnight. Khuon and Sah wanted to tag along with me. Sah said that we could go our separate ways once we reached Phnom Penh. He claimed that he knew the way back to Koh Thom, his hometown. Khuon did not want to return to Pursat; he wanted to stay with me. We were over a hundred kilometers from the capital. Together, the three of us walked along the highway. We waved at the oncoming trucks, asking for a ride. Few trucks stopped for us, and those that did moved on without us, the drivers not willing to give us a ride, as we did not have the fare.

We finally got a ride after about five kilometers of walking. The truck's destination was the capital of Kompong Thom. It was late in the afternoon when we arrived in the city. We went to the city hall to ask for food and a place to sleep. After dinner, I walked around the city and asked truck drivers if we could get a ride to Phnom Penh. One driver said that he would be leaving for Prek Kdam at noon. Prek Kdam, or Crab Canal, is not too far from Phnom Penh. We could walk from there to Phnom Penh in not much time. I was very anxious to get back to my hometown.

I woke up early in the morning, and we began to walk. The driver, who had told me he would leave at noon, caught us around Skun's area. He laughed as he saw us, and he gave us a ride all the way to Prek Kdam. We took a boat across the river, and we continued to walk to Phnom Penh. We spent the night six kilometers short of Phnom Penh.

\* \* \*

Phnom Penh was like a ghost town. We walked to Watt Phnom and along Norodom Boulevard toward Kbal Thnal. I was very excited. Since this was the first time Sah and Khuon were in Phnom Penh, I was their tour guide. I told them that my father used to take me to Watt Phnom on his days off to play on the swings. I remembered the time when I saw the giant bones of the dolphin in Watt Phnom Museum. I pointed out toward the Red Bank, where I was told that the money was made. Then we went to Lycee Sisowath, "This is one of our rivals" I told them with a smile.

I pointed out the back gate of the palace, and then we were in front of the former Minister of Education's building. We took a short break there. I told Sah and Khuon of my participation in demonstrations and the one where we took the two ministers into custody. I did not want to think about it, but the old memories kept coming back.

We walked around Independence Monument, where Norodom and Sihanouk Boulevards crossed, and kept going on Norodom Boulevard. We reached the pharmacy on Chrun Yu Hak Street. I stopped there for a moment to tell the boys that, along this sidewalk, there used to be many book vendors.

"I spent most of my spare time here, reading books," I recalled. "Toward the end of the street, there are many big buildings where people used to live. I stayed with my friend, Dok, in the second building. If you keep going east, you will see many huts along the Basac River. One of them was my house. I built it with my father and my brother-in-law for our family." We kept on moving.

I pointed out the old United States Embassy. Then we reached Chamkar Mon, where Prince Sihanouk used to stay. General Lon Nol had used it for an office after he deposed the prince. An air force pilot had dropped a bomb here to try to kill General Lon Nol. I was told that the pilot defected to join the prince and the Khmer Rouge. I pointed to the place where the republic government had placed a rocket to shoot down planes if they attempted to drop bombs again.

Next to Chamkar Mon was Lycee Chak Angre. My brother, Samith, had gone to this school, while I had attended Lycee Tuol Svay Prey, formerly known as Chao Pornhea Yath. The Khmer Rouge had changed the name of my Lycee to Tuol Sleng. They had used my high school as their prison.

Samoeurn in 1993 at Tuol Sleng

We arrived at the warehouse where Dok and I had found the rice just a few months into the rule of the Communist regime. I remembered building the raft and bringing rice to our families.

Sometimes, we saw people run across the boulevard. We saw Vietnamese soldiers guarding the mansions along the boulevard. The soldiers stopped us a couple of times so they could search our bags. We told them that we had nothing except a small amount of food supplies and that we wanted to get to Chroy Ampil Thmey, to my uncle's home. We did not have any problems passing through Phnom Penh.

We arrived in Kbal Thnal around noon. This was where Highway Routes 1 and 2 split. Sah told me that he knew how to get to his hometown from here. I asked him to come with me to my uncle's house first, since it was only about eight or nine kilometers away. His hometown was twenty kilometers away. I promised to take him home once I had learned my family's situation. Sah was anxious to get home. He thanked me and requested to go separate ways. I knew Sah was smart. He had learned tricks during our journey, and I believed that he would not be harmed traveling alone. I had no choice but to let him go. We went our separate ways. Sah took Highway Route 2 to Koh Thom. Khuon and I crossed Monivong's bridge toward Highway Route 1 to Chroy Ampil, Kbal Koh.

I was looking for my aunt and uncle in my hometown. I was worried that they might not have survived the Khmer Rouge regime, since they were not at our family's plot. My distant cousin told me that the Khmer Rouge had moved them about two kilometers east of here. They had never left town.

I hurried to get to their home. My uncle was extremely happy to see me. He was very sad when I told him that his younger brother, my father, had passed away. My uncle's family was intact. He had not lost any children. Instead, he'd had another son during the revolution.

My uncle lived in a house above the ground. Under his house was stock of rice. The family did a little farming to support their seven children. My uncle told me that I was his only nephew who had survived and had been able to make his way back home. He wanted me to stay with him and wait for other family members to reunite. He welcomed Khuon into the family.

I went to visit the in-laws of my eldest sister in Khum Dey Eth, about nine kilometers from Chroy Ampil, looking for my sister. I learned that my oldest sister and her husband had been executed in Battambang, on the west side of Pursat Province. Three of their daughters had died of starvation and disease. The village people had adopted the last one, who was still alive.

My mother, my sisters, and my brothers were still trapped with the Khmer Rouge somewhere in Pursat.

Every morning, we got up early, took out enough rice grains for our meal, and separated the rice from the skin. My uncle's eldest son, Sophal, Khuon, and I would go to the lake after lunch to fish. The fish became harder to catch as time went by. More people were fishing than there were fish in the lake. The stockpile of rice got lower and lower, and the situation became tougher and tougher. My uncle had great difficulty providing for his children.

In addition to this burden, my aunt, who was my mother's sister, her husband, and their four children had moved in. I did everything I could to help out. But the situation did not get any better.

One night, I overheard my aunt and uncle complaining about the shortage of food. My aunt felt that I was not contributing enough to alleviate the family's needs. My uncle tried to defend me, but as usual, he surrendered and kept quiet. I understood why my aunt felt the way she felt. I felt lonely and unwanted.

I determined to stand up on my own. I left them a note, telling my family not to worry about me, packed up my belongings, and left. I went to the west bank to look for my second brother-in-law's family. Brother Samon was very happy to see me. He was very sad to hear that Sareth, his brother, had died. "If he had listened and come here when I had asked him to, he would still be alive," Samon lamented.

Samon and his wife told me that I could stay with them as long as I wanted. Their eldest son, who was a couple of years younger than me, was married and lived next door. They took me out farming and fishing. These were the jobs I knew best since my time with the Communists. When we did not fish or farm, his wife, his daughter, and I would go to cut *kark* (tall grasses) to make mats that we would sell at the open market. I was very happy to work as a farmer. Compared to my life under the Communist regime, this was heaven. I did not desire any kind of change and thought that I would get married and settle down in the west bank.

\* \* \*

The rest of my immediate family was able to get away from the Khmer Rouge around June or July of 1979. My mother, Savath, Samuth, Savan, Phalla, and Ravy returned to our hometown. They learned that I had stayed with my uncle for less than a month and left. My family was sad. My aunt and uncle told them that they had looked for me all over the place. My mother told them that she did not worry too much about me. She was sure that I was safe and that I would be back when I was ready.

My mother stayed with my aunt and uncle while she looked for a place to live. Meanwhile, my mother and my sister worked a small business to support the family. After about a month, my sister asked my mother if she could visit her brother-in-law, Samon. She wanted to give him the news about her husband, who the Communists had killed.

She arrived at Samon's with her daughter, Ravy, and was very surprised to find me there. She thanked her brother-in-law for taking me in and asked to bring me home. Brother Samon was happy to see my sister and his only niece, Ravy. He said that it was up to me whether I wanted to go back to Chroy Ampil. Of course I wanted to go. I had not seen my family for months.

My mother told me that my brother, Samith, had joined the government military after he left the Khmer Rouge. He was doing well in the forces and held a high-ranking position. His post was in Pursat.

The capital, Phnom Penh, reopened for people to return. By the time I rejoined the family, another family had moved into our home. My mother wanted to go back to the city where she could run her small business. There was no land to farm in Chroy Ampil. Plus, all the land was occupied.

I went back to Phnom Penh to look for a place for us to live. Most houses were taken, and those that were not occupied had already been claimed by someone else. I finally found a place for us in Chbar Ampeu District, on the east side of the Basac River. I told the family that it was a temporary place for us while I looked for a permanent home in the city.

# CHAPTER 26

# New Life Struggle

My mother told me that when she had left the Communists, she had a couple of buffalo and a buffalo cart. She had traded them for gold. She also had some gold left over from trading during the Khmer Rouge time. For the first few months of the new regime, there still was no currency in use. We traded gold for necessities. Rice was another commodity for trade. With her gold as capital, my mother was able to set up a small table close to Chbar Ampeu market to sell rice soup. My sister also helped by making dessert to sell. My mother gave me about an ounce of gold to start my own business.

I met with Kim Loeung and Tong Kheng, my former classmates, to discuss a business plan. Kim Loeung said that the village he had been in during the Khmer Rouge was short of tobacco but had lots of brown sugar. As sugar was very valuable in Phnom Penh, we should try to make a deal there. Cambodia did not have much tobacco after the Khmer Rouge regime. So Kim Loeung, Tong Kheng, and I made a trip to Vietnam. Tong Kheng had a hundred-dollar bill for capital. It was the first time I had seen a hundred-dollar bill. Kim Loeung had a little gold sheet that his sister had given him. I still had my ounce of gold.

We rode a bike to Vietnam from Phnom Penh. We asked people who lived along the highway if we could stay with them for the night. On one of the nights, Kim Loeung slept with the lady of the house. Tong Kheng was very upset. We were on a business trip, and Tong Kheng and I believed that Kim Loeung's indiscretion would bring us bad luck. I was also uncomfortable hearing Kim Loeung boast about his lovemaking the night before. We continued our journey to Vietnam to buy tobacco.

We went along with a group of people who made frequent trips to Vietnam to do business. We were new to this border-crossing business. Vietnamese soldiers arrested the three of us right before we crossed the border. While under arrest, Tong Kheng and I remained silent. Unaware that we could bribe the border patrol to secure our release, we quietly contemplated how we could get out of this mess.

But not Kim Loeung. "You cannot arrest me," he told the soldiers. "I did nothing wrong. I am standing on Cambodian ground, not your land. You have no right to arrest me."

"Are you sure you are on your land?" said the soldier, pushing his pistol against Kim Loeung's head.

Kim Loeung's face turned pale, almost a violet color.

Tong Kheng and I were still quiet.

Kim Loeung begged, "No, sir, it is your land. I am sorry, sir; I am sorry. Here is my gold. Take it. Please don't kill me."

The soldier smiled. He took the gold and let us go. We crossed the border into the first Vietnamese town. Tong Kheng and I traded our gold and hundred-dollar bill for Vietnamese currency. While we were on the way to the market, the soldiers chased us again. We ran into a Vietnamese house. The household hid us in their mosquito net. The family asked us for some money to bribe the soldiers to go away. We heard them converse in Vietnamese, and then the soldiers left. The villager told us that we could not go to the market with the bike. The soldiers were on both ends of the bridge to the market. They offered us a boat ride to the market. We took the boat ride and bought as much tobacco as we could with the money we had left.

Kim Loeung took us to the village he'd lived in to trade for sugar. The farmers did not have as much sugar as they'd had the previous year due to the recent war. We brought the little sugar they had with the tobacco. We had lost lots of capital on this trip.

My mother told me to stay home. She felt that business was not for me. "You should go to Pursat to see your brother. Maybe Samith could find you a government job there. We do not know anyone here. Finding a government job here is hard."

I agreed with my mother. That was the last time I saw my mother and my family.

# CHAPTER 27

# Life in the Guerrilla Camp

I was glad to see Samith in uniform, serving the country. I told him that our mother wanted me to work here with him. He said that he did not believe that the current government could withstand the pressure from the West. He had heard from people who had traveled to the border to get merchandise from Thailand that there were some resistance armies along the border. There were several factions, and the Khmer Rouge was one of them. However, he said that the other groups sounded very nationalistic. He wanted me to check them out. He asked me to leave Phalla with him. I agreed, and I went west without any money.

I asked for a ride from people who biked to the border and got a ride to Battambang. After the bikers dropped me off in the city, I ate the food that was left over from the bag that my mother had packed for me and went to sleep on the sidewalk. I woke up early in the morning and continued to walk toward the border. Along the way, I met a family who had lived in our village during the Khmer Rouge regime. They told me that they were on their way to the border. They stopped frequently since they had small children. I left them and hurried to the border. I would later meet the same family in Long Beach, California.

I spent the night at the home of a government soldier before crossing the border to the nationalistic guerrilla camps. The soldier's wife was home while her husband was out to work that evening. She told me that most people who came through here had a bike and a bag and were on their way to Thailand to buy goods. She did not believe I was one of them. "I know you are going to a guerrilla camp. If my husband were here, he would have arrested you. He does not like those border guerrillas. You must plan to join the guerrillas.

Why don't you eat now and go to sleep? Do not say anything. I will take care of him," she said with a smile.

Per her request, I did not say anything. I trusted her. I ate and went to sleep on the bed under her house with other travelers. I woke up in the middle of the night and left with a group of people, after thanking the soldier's wife. The group grew larger and larger as we traveled. Each one of us traveled for one of two purposes—to seek refuge in a camp or to buy goods from Thailand and return to make money in Cambodia. We walked all night on the muddy roads. We took a break at dawn. We continued to walk again through the woods. We had to be very careful. We could not wander off the path, or we might step on a minefield, buried by either one of the guerilla factions or the government.

I arrived in the border camp of Thailand at midnight. I slept on the wet ground. That evening I went to sleep with an empty stomach. I was intensely hungry. When I woke up, I went to look for food in the neighborhood huts. The people told me to join the guerrilla's forces to get food.

Before I knew it, I became a guerrilla soldier in the camp. I sent notes to my brother to explain what I was doing in the guerrilla camp and what camp life was like. I did not know whether or not my letter would get through to him. I probably was the only untrained soldier in the camp. I carried an M-16 shotgun, and I didn't know how to shoot it. I had never liked guns anyway. I was asked to guard the rice stock throughout the night. I often felt asleep with my gun in my arms and lost it when I awoke. My commander, who seemed to understand my dilemma, was the one who had taken the gun away from me when I was sleeping on duty. Luckily, I was never punished. He usually gave my gun back the following day.

One evening, while I was swinging on my hammock, singing to myself, the cook handed me a note from the commander's daughter. After I read it, I gave back to her.

"Aunty, this note is not for me," I told her. "There is no name on the note. It is probably for Chantha. He is on the other side of the rice stock."

Aunt Mab bent down and whispered in my ear. "She told me to give it to you. You should do what she asks."

I was struck with disbelief, and then I returned to reality. I tore the note after I had reread it, as the letter had instructed me to do. I asked Aunt Mab to leave so that I could gather myself and think through what was happening. I was scared, confused, and nervous. I searched my heart and head, trying to understand why I had received the note. The only explanation I could come up with was that, perhaps, the commander's daughter felt sorry for me. Again, I reasoned that the cook may have made a mistake.

I was validated the next morning when I received a gift and a ten-dollar bill from the commander's other daughter, her younger sister. It was the first time in my life that I had touched a ten-dollar bill. *It looks somewhat like the hundred-dollar bill Tong Kheng had a couple months ago*, I said to myself.

I went to the market and bought my first pair of jeans ever. Although I had no feelings for the commander's daughter in the beginning, her kindness and daily gifts began to plant a seed of love in my heart. Was I being bought? I did not know. Before I knew it, I was fully in love with her. For a normal American, this love may seem a strange love. Although my love and I lived in the same compound, we never talked to one another. However, we wrote each other many times a day. As usual, we destroyed our notes after we had read them. We secretly gave each other smiles. Our secret messengers were the cook and my love's little sister.

Early in November 1979, the Phnom Penh government shot rockets into our camp. The guerrilla troupe was no match for the Vietnamese and the government soldiers. We ran across the border to Thailand. We stayed in the temple, waiting for the fighting to settle down. November 11, 1979, the Khao I Dang (KID) refugee camp opened. Khao I Dang as I was told by the Thai means "Mountain I Dang." The camp was located at the bottom of I Dang Mountain. Many people in the temple and the camp sought refuge at Khao I Dang.

I was lost in the guerrilla camp. Aunty Mab came to tell me that the commander's daughter insisted that I go with her family to the refugee camp, "She is worried that you might be killed in the camp," the cook told me.

I was touched by her concern, and I agreed to go along. After a couple months in the refugee camp, the commander's daughter dumped me for my friend. I was upset at first and, later, felt that fate must have stepped in. She and I were not meant to be together. I was okay with that.

A few months later, I received a note from Uncle Ann, who lived in the guerrilla camp. He told me that my mother was in the guerrilla camp looking for me. When Uncle Ann told her that I had gone to the refugee camp, she'd said she wanted me to keep going west. She wanted me to pursue a higher education and return to help my siblings.

I regretted that I had missed her, but I remembered my parents' words: "Properties can be burned, stolen, or taken away, but no one can take education away from you." The Pol Pot regime proved my parents right. We all lost everything, except our heads.

# CHAPTER 28

# Refugee Camps

I had always been fascinated with the traditional dances of Cambodia, especially folk dances. When I was in Phnom Penh, I used to go to watch the dance practice at the fine arts school. I would go home and practice what I had seen, singing and dancing.

I joined the dance group when the group came to the camp to recruit new members. I was told that, as a Khmer cultural dancer, I would have a better chance of going to a third country.

I was good at it. We practiced day and night and put on several shows a week. In addition to dancing, I volunteered to work in the tuberculosis ward. Due to the busy schedule with the dance group, I was not able to keep up with my job in the hospital. For the sake of my health and that of others who I cared for at the ward, the ward chief asked me to make a decision—either work full-time in the hospital or stay with the dance group. I chose to stay with the dance group. I was glad that the ward chief had given me a choice, since quitting the dance group was not an option for me. I liked to keep myself busy.

During one of my many dance performances, my name was called. I turned to see where the call had come from. I was happy to see my best friend, Tong Kheng, and his brother Tong Beng. I met with him after the performance.

"When did you get here?" I asked. "Are you with your family?"

Tong Kheng laughed before he responded. "I didn't know that you could dance," he told me. "I am glad to see you. I get here last month, with Tong Beng only."

Tong Kheng told me that he had found his sister, who was currently living in Seattle. His sister had already completed the sponsorship paperwork for him and Tong Beng.

"If you do not have anyone to sponsor you, I could ask my sister to sponsor you too," he added.

"Really?" I exclaimed. "That is great Tong Kheng. I joined the Khmer folk dance group because I was told that we would have a better chance of being sponsored to a third country. It would be wonderful if you and your sister could do that for me."

Presently, Tong Kheng is still living in Seattle and is working for the Boeing Company as a mechanical engineer. His brother, Tong Beng, moved to Boston and established a successful business there.

One of the highlights of that time was when our dance group was invited to perform at the Miss Thai pageant in Phanatnikhom, Chonburi. We were bused out of the camp. The pageant coordinators fed us good food.

Coconut Dance in Khao I Dang Refugee Camp (1979);
(from left to right in back) Hong, Sreng, Arun, Sam, and Mony;
(from left to right in front) Tey, Mom, Maly, Thoeun, and Khan

After a few months in the camp, people started to leave for third countries. I asked people how I could leave the refugee camp to go to a developed country, since I had heard no news about the dance group's chance to relocate. To increase my chances of being selected, I wrote my autobiography, with the help of friends who translated it to English, and sent my resettlement application to the embassies of all the countries that accepted refugees.

I was fortunate that many Western countries, including France, Belgium, Switzerland, New Zealand, the United Kingdom, Australia, West Germany, the United States, Canada, and even Japan accepted my petition for resettlement in their country. On July 13, 1980, my name was selected to go to a transit camp. I waited for completion of the process of resettlement in the United States. I taught myself additional English and practiced through volunteer work with the humanitarian workers. I taught my fellow refugees English as well. The teaching encouraged me to read more and to practice my English more.

I was involved with a woman who lived next to the hut I was teaching at. Our relationship was like that of a boyfriend and girlfriend. She was a widow with two children and was a couple of years older than me, but that did not bother me.

While I waited for the final interview, I received several notes from my girlfriend, who told me how much she missed me and that she could not live without me. She claimed that she had jewelry and other assets and that we could be better off by going back to Cambodia, using her assets for capital to start a business. I missed her, and I was afraid that she might kill herself if I left. In addition, going back to Cambodia did not sound so bad. I was here alone struggling, while all my siblings and my mother were still in Phnom Penh. I also heard, by word of mouth, that if I told the immigration agent that I had a wife in the KID, the agent would bring her along to America. So I did.

My interviewer was upset. "You lied to me. You did not tell me that you were married in the first interview. We do not approve liars in America. In your original document, you said you were single and had no family."

I was very sad about my mistake and angry that I was not able to speak proper English to explain the reason behind my claim. I withdrew myself completely from friends and others. A Japanese nun who I had befriended came to visit me and told me that, if I still wanted to go to a third country, she would work to get me to Japan. I refused to go anywhere but the United States or back to Cambodia. I felt that I would be better off going back to see my family in Phnom Penh.

My girlfriend was happy that I did not leave. I finally decided that I should go back home. I went to the United Nations High Commissioner for Refugees, also known as UNHCR, to request a return to KID. Many of my close friends were against my plan. They told me to move on to a third country.

"Love is blind. I am sure that when you get to the third country, you will forget her," said Meng Hong, one of my friends, who currently lives in Fort Worth, Texas. He owns a gas station and a liquor store.

July 15, 1980, Meng Hong and Samoeurn
Phanatnikhom, Chonburi Refugee Camp

I refused to listen to my friends. The UNHCR put me on the bus back to the KID in September 1980. While I was on the bus back, I told myself that, as soon as I got back to the KID, I would go back to Cambodia with my girlfriend and her two children to begin my life there.

My girlfriend was very happy to see me back. She came to greet me and took me to her home.

I was anxious as I entered the home. I asked her to get ready to go back to Cambodia. But she had different plans. "No. We do not have to go back," she told me. "My family is in France and will sponsor us. We should be called soon to go to France. I do not want to return to Cambodia."

"In every note you sent me, you said that our life would be better together when I returned. You said that we could start our business in Cambodia with the gold you have. Was it a lie?" I asked.

"No, it was not a lie," she responded tearfully. "It's just that we still have a chance to go to a third country together. My sister and my father-in-law are in France. They are working very hard to get us there. Please be patient."

"Be patient?" I responded angrily. "I gave up a golden opportunity to go to America to come back to you so that we could build a new life together. You told me that you have capital for a business. Where is it? Was that a lie too?" I was upset. I showered and took a nap to calm myself.

When I woke up, my girlfriend showed me the golden necklace. She said that, if I truly wanted to go back to Cambodia, we could start with this small bit of capital. I was beyond mad. I recognized the necklace. It belonged to her friend. I confronted her. She was very emotional. She pulled out a pair of scissors and cut the necklace into pieces. I thought she was stupid and crazy. She claimed that her friend had borrowed her necklace and had just returned it. I told myself that I couldn't live with this woman. I began to put in another petition to go to a third country.

I must be the luckiest refugee I know. My name was posted on the bulletin board for the INS interview to go to America the following month. This time, I was careful to make sure that I was clear that I wanted to go to America.

My girlfriend knew that I would leave her for sure this time. She entered the interview room, crying. She told the interviewer that I was her husband and that she would like to come along. I was beyond mad. I kept my mouth shut and let her do the talking. The interviewer felt sorry for her. He told her that he would make another case for her to come along. He suggested that I go to the transit camp to wait for her there.

I was sent to a transit camp in Phanatnikhom, Chonburi, where I waited for my visa. I found myself with lots of time to think. I had been lied to by a woman I'd planned to spend my whole life with, and I had almost lost a chance to go to America. The more I thought, the madder I got. Without thinking of the consequences, I informed the INS agent that my wife had left for France, and I gave them her name to file on record. Lo and behold, a month later, the INS brought my girlfriend and her two children to the transit camp and combined the two cases.

My case appeared messy again. I did not have an explanation for what I had said. The INS agent told me that USA did not allow polygamy. It appeared that I had more than one wife. If I wanted to go to America, I needed to have only one wife. To facilitate the case, Meng Hong convinced my girlfriend to file for a divorce at the UNHCR, claiming that I had been unfaithful. So she did, and our cases were separated.

Chonburi Camp, October 1980; (from left to right) Nuphear, Samoeurn, Tong Kheng, and Tong Beng

While I waited for the transition to America, I volunteered to work at the Catholic Relief Services, also known as CRS. Working for Mr. Somsak and Mr. Jon Howell, I taught folk dances to the younger refugees. Mr. Somsak and Mr. Howell gave me a small salary so that I could buy my personal needs, such as shampoo, soap, a toothbrush, and toothpaste. Our dance group performed almost weekly; sometimes we performed for the distinguished guests who came to visit the camp, and other times we were just entertaining our fellow refugees.

On February 21, 1981, I flew to Singapore, and then I took a boat to Galang Island in Indonesia. I arrived in a new transit camp, where refugees were taught to get themselves ready to start life in America. My girlfriend flew to this same island a couple of weeks later. I tried to distance myself from her in order to avoid trouble. I volunteered to work as an English teacher's aide with one of the Indonesian teachers. For me, that was a way of learning the language without going to school. I was able to make friends with the Indonesians and practice English with them. Since I was a good ping-pong player, Santeo, one of the teachers, took me to his dorm every weekend to play ping-pong with him. We became good friends.

# CHAPTER 29

# Coming to America

I took a boat to Singapore on May 25, 1981, to prepare the paperwork so that I could go to America. Santeo and four of the Indonesian teachers had taken me out for a good-bye lunch the day before.

On May 28, I left Singapore to travel to America. I dressed in a thin, short-sleeved shirt, long pants, and sandals, which a refugee in Singapore had given me. In my handbag, I carried a notebook and a pen. Those clothes and that bag were all I had when I left for America. On the plane, I was fascinated to see the sun rise twice in one day. It was freezing cold on the plane. Cold air blew at me from above and the below; I thought that there were leaks in the plane. The flight attendant came by and saw me shivering; with both feet on the seat, I embraced my knees to keep myself warm. She left and returned with a small blanket. I was so grateful for her kindness. I covered myself with the blanket after thanking her. Later, she came back with hot tea. I wanted to show her my gratitude for her kindness.

"Miss, what is your name?" I asked.

"Lori," she replied with a smile.

"What is your address?" I said, as I pulled out my notebook.

She chuckled. "I am married," she responded.

I was confused. I wanted to know her address so I could pay her back for her kindness. Why had she told me she was married? Years later, I found out that my question was probably intrusive.

My first flight to the United States was the longest flight I have ever been on. As I looked down, I saw many houses and buildings on the hills. *There are no rice fields*, I thought. *Where am I going to get rice to eat?* I was sad and worried. Because of my limited English, I was scared that I would not survive in this country. I wanted to go back home.

The plane arrived at the San Francisco International Airport about noon. I was reluctant to get off of the plane. A Vietnamese translator arrived to speak to us refugees. He talked to us in Vietnamese, which I didn't understand, but I was able to pick up a few words in English when he translated. I learned that all of us had a sponsor and not all the sponsors were here. Many of us had sponsors in other states. We must wait for our assignment. I was nervous. I paced back and forth anxiously.

It was almost 3:00 p.m., and many of the refugees had already left. Only a small group of us stayed behind. I finally had the courage to approach the translator.

"When do we go?" I asked him

"I don't know," he told me. "Sit down and wait." Then he proceeded to speak to the Vietnamese refugees.

I thought that he was being rude. I kept asking him more questions.

"Can you ask them when we can go?"

The translator got mad at me. He turned to a Vietnamese refugee and walked away. He spoke to himself, loudly enough so that I could hear, "Stupid Cambodian."

I was upset, but I kept my cool.

At around 4:00 p.m., our group was called to board the plane, a 747 Pan Am, for a nonstop flight to New York. I tried to rest as much as I could.

When the pilot announced that the plane was to land at JFK shortly, I saw through my window bright lights shining from the ground. I was so excited. A tear rolled down my cheek. *This must be what paradise looks like. Yes, I'm in heaven*, I thought.

It was about midnight in New York, and it was still sprinkling after a heavy rain. I was cold when I got off the plane. I saw a couple of Vietnamese people who held a sign with my name on it. I went up to them and showed them the documents that the INS had given me. They asked if I had any luggage. When I said no, they smiled at each other. They walked me to the parking lot. I was like a little bird with wet wings. They tried to cover me with an umbrella to protect me from getting wet. I was scared. I had the stereotypical beliefs that Vietnamese and Cambodians didn't get along. I thought they would treat me badly. There was a lot on my mind as I walked to the car and sat in the backseat.

We merged onto the highway and continued to downtown Manhattan. The couple talked to each other the whole way home. Once in a while, they would ask how I was doing. I didn't answer them because I was too busy looking around. I was like a monkey entering the city, with my eyes opened wide. Now I was wide awake. I was looking for bicyclists or motorcyclists. Out of curiosity, I put my broken English together and said, "No bicycle; no motorcycle. I cannot see."

They looked at me, then at each other, and exploded in friendly laughter. "No, no motorcycle. It's raining," they told me.

Before long, we got to their apartment. I don't know what floor they lived on. I only remember that we went into the elevator.

As they opened the apartment door, I saw a television set, a sofa, and a love seat. The floor was made of wood. It was weird to me, since we were in a high-rise apartment. How could anyone build a house floor with wood when it was so high off the ground? I expected to see tiles or a marble floor, like in buildings in Cambodia.

The couple showed me the restroom and how to flush the toilet. They brought me night clothes to change into. They pulled out the sofa bed and said, "You'll sleep here tonight."

Then I saw a young boy, probably eight or ten years old, coming out of the room. He spoke to them. I didn't understand, but I guessed he was talking about me since he pointed at me several times. I went to the bathroom to change. I tried to figure out how to use the shower or take a bath. The water was either too hot or too cold. I gave up on my desire to bathe myself and went to the toilet. I stared at it for a while. I finally climbed up with my feet on the seat to do my business.

The woman woke me up in the morning. She asked why I hadn't bathed last night. I told her that I did not know how to use the shower. She went in with me and turned on the water for me.

When I came out of the bathroom, I saw her son at the breakfast table with a school uniform and backpack on. I had bread and bacon for breakfast. She asked me to dress up.

"We are ready to go," she said.

She shook her head when I pulled out my shirt and pants to wear. She went to her husband's closet and took out clothes for me to try on. They were all too big for me. I told her I was okay with the large outfit. In fact, I was happy and thankful. I thought that she was very kind, and indeed she was kind. It was cold, so I wore three layers of shirts and two layers of pants. She took one pair of her husband's shoes and asked me to try them on. All of them were too big, either size 9 or 10. I wore size 8. It didn't matter to me. I was thankful. I put toilet paper into the tip of the shoes so they would fit. With this outfit, I walked out of the house looking like a penguin. I sat in the backseat while the boy sat next to his mother. He talked nonstop with his mother until he got to school.

As a new immigrant, I was shocked and excited by everything. After dropping off the boy at his school, the woman drove me to the International Rescue Committee (IRC) on Park Ave. I was glad that the IRC agency was sponsoring me. In the refugee camp, the IRC was well respected, and I had worked for them as well. The woman introduced me to a Cambodian caseworker and told me that he had been assigned to me. She then went into the office. I thought she must be the boss of the agency.

I followed the caseworker, whose name I don't recall, to his cubicle. He told me that his wife also worked for the agency. After gathering all my background information and work history, he had me sign a few documents and gave me my social security card and my I-94. He told me that I needed both of them to work. He asked me what I wanted to do. I found him trustworthy and sincere. And knowing that New York City was a big city, I knew I was lucky to meet a Khmer caseworker.

Without hesitation, I told him that I wanted to go to school.

He appeared surprised. He probably didn't expect that type of response. "Brother, America did not bring you here to go through school and become their boss. They brought you here to work."

I was disappointed. I could not help but push the issue. "But I heard you can go to school when you come to America," I insisted.

My caseworker looked at me and talked in a cold, low tone. "Listen, you will not amount to anything but a slave here to the Americans."

I kept my mouth shut before I got into any more trouble. My Cambodian caseworker placed me with a Chinese Cambodian couple who lived in a one-bedroom apartment in China Town. The couple spoke little Khmer, mostly conversing in Chinese. Both got up early to go to work in China Town and came home late in the evening. I barely saw them.

Three days after I moved in, my caseworker came by and asked me to pack my stuff. He moved me in with a Cambodian family who lived in a basement in Manhattan. He found me a job in Manhattan, working in a Japanese restaurant. My position in this "Nippon" restaurant was split. For the first half of my shift, I washed the dishes, and for the second half, I packed food for Japan Airlines. I worked the graveyard shift, eight hours per day, putting in overtime two to three times per week. The family I lived with found me an adult school to attend. I spent three hours in class a day, and the class ended at 9:00 p.m. I usually stayed around the library or at the restaurant to do my homework or read my notes until my shift began at midnight. Working overtime cut down my sleeping time tremendously, but I always felt that the job was much easier than anything I had endured under the Khmer Rouge and that I could do this forever. I used my weekends off to rest as much as I could.

Saturday, July 4, 1981, American Independence Day, was a memorable day for me. No one had told me how Americans celebrated their Independence Day or even told me that it was a holiday. All I saw were American flags waving everywhere. When the fireworks began, I lay on the floor between the bed and the wall to protect myself from the bullets. I was on the floor even before the big fireworks began. I was in my apartment when the kids in the neighborhood started playing with fireworks, and when I heard the popping sounds, I thought that America was at war and fighting had broken out everywhere in New York.

I had many friends in different states, and I called them every weekend to keep in touch. I also made one American friend in New York, Jeff. Jeff told me that he was an engineer. He lived in Manhattan with his Japanese girlfriend. One night, he invited me to his apartment for dinner with him and his girlfriend. He came to pick me up. I don't remember exactly what floor he lived on, but the apartment was on a high floor near Times Square. It was a one-bedroom apartment with breathtaking views. His girlfriend prepared food while Jeff and I were on the balcony talking. I couldn't help but ask him a question.

"How much is the rent, Jeff?"

"Fifteen hundred dollars," he replied.

"Fifteen hundred dollars!" I shouted. My minimum wage pay was $3.35 per hour.

"Your rent is about three times my monthly income. I could never afford this," I said skeptically.

"You are good with math, Sam. You should be an engineer."

I was happy to hear his praise. "But I want to be a doctor. I want to take care of sick people."

He nodded his head, "Yes, you could. In America, you can be anything you want to be, as long as you work hard toward your goal."

Jeff's words were the complete opposite of those of my caseworker. I was fortunate to be friends with him. He was kind and considerate.

After three months working the graveyard shift at the restaurant, I became very ill. I was unable to go to work due to a high fever. At that time, I had already moved in with a friend of mine, Sokun Reach, in Brooklyn. Sokun's family included his wife, his baby, and his brother, Palla. We lived in a one-bedroom apartment where Church Avenue and Ocean Avenue crossed. His brother and I slept in the living room.

Sokun took me to King's Hospital. I was not admitted but was prescribed antibiotics for my fever. When I got better, I went to look for a day job. Since I did not have skills and resources, looking for a job in New York City was not easy. I made a phone call to Uncle Chhan, a refugee I knew from the KID refugee camp. He assured me that he could help me with school and a job if I moved to Ohio, where he lived. I was excited to hear the options he told me about.

I went to say good-bye to Jeff. Jeff tried to convince me to stay in New York. He said he would help me find a job, adding that I could continue to attend adult school until my English was good enough to go to college. But I had already made up my mind. I was too eager to attend college and to have the Khmer guidance of Uncle Chhan. Unable to persuade me to stay, Jeff bought me a plane ticket to Cleveland. I left New York from La Guardia Airport. Besides paying for my plane ticket, Jeff took me to the airport to be sure that I was not late for my flight. "Thank you, Jeff," I said solemnly.

I got to Cleveland in late September 1981. The city was tranquil compared to New York City. However, the Cambodian families were busy. They often met after work and on the weekend to drink and watch football. Since I did not drink and I did not know how to watch football, I was kind of an outcast. With Uncle Chhan's direction, I took a bus to Cuyahoga Community College in Cleveland to attempt to enroll for school. The school had already been in session since early September. The counselor gave me a placement test, and I was supposed to be placed in intermediate algebra and an ESL class. But I had to wait till the spring semester. I took this opportunity to get to know the community and to look for a job.

A week passed by, and I still had not found a job. I called a friend, Sina Bou, in Philadelphia to see how he was doing. Sina told me that I should move there.

"You do not have to work and you can go to school full-time," Sina Bou told me. "The government pays for our living expenses. You can also start from high school here, if you want."

That was good news to me. I knew that I had a strong accent. I thought that if I went to high school with younger kids, I would learn English better. Going to school full-time without having to work sounded extremely good to me. I explained to Uncle Chhan what Sina had told me and my plan to move on. Uncle Chhan also knew Sina from the camp. He understood why I wanted to leave, and he wished me luck. I politely said good-bye to him and hopped on the Greyhound bus to Philadelphia.

Sina came to greet me at the bus station. He took me on the subway to his apartment in West Philadelphia. He lived with his brother, Sida, in a studio apartment on Walnut Street, between 42nd and 43rd Streets. Their apartment was situated very conveniently. Alpha Beta Supermarket was right across the street. The refugee service center and welfare office were about a half mile away. Refugees also received help from the National Service Center in downtown Philadelphia. University of Pennsylvania was a few blocks east.

I moved in with Sina and his brother. Our shared rent was low, but it was still difficult for us to meet our daily needs. To reduce the rent and utilities costs, Sina moved in three more friends—Thay Ros, Vannak Por, and a Cambodian Chinese guy whose name I've forgotten—into the apartment. We each paid Sina forty dollars for rent and utilities. Altogether, there were six single men in a studio apartment. Because of the tight space, we all put our mattresses on the floor to sleep. In addition to the six of us, Ky and Phoy, a couple of Cambodian Laotian guys who each lived with their single mothers, came to spend time and to sleep with us on the weekends.

Sam and Sina in Philadelphia, 1982

In addition to Ky and Phoy, Sina also had three American friends who came to visit him regularly. Tim was an older American fellow of Italian descendent. He usually brought us food and took us to church. We enjoyed going to different churches and he had exposed us to a number of different churches. For Thanksgivings 1981, he took us to Brooklyn, my old neighborhood, to join in the holiday celebration at the Cambodian Church on Ocean Boulevard. He introduced us to the Italian Market in Philadelphia. Tim was also responsible for getting Sina and I baptized at a Baptist church in South Philadelphia.

He did not mind spending the night with us on the floor once in a while.

1981 Halloween party, South Philadelphia Baptist Church,
(standing from left, Tim, Sida, Samoeurn, and Ky (I have forgotten the names
of the rest of the group); (kneeling in front of Sida) Ros Thai

Jeff was another Caucasian friend of Sina's. A college student, Jeff spoke Cambodian and had a Cambodian girlfriend. He later married her and moved to Seattle, Washington. Jeff usually came to our apartment with a guitar. He taught Sina how to play musical instruments and took me for a driving lesson once. We drove his father's car. He asked me to follow the car in front of us, and I did so literally, even when the car turned at a red light. I almost ran into two or three cars. Jeff was screaming at the top of his lungs from the passenger seat. I was scared. He asked me to move to the passenger seat, and we returned home. Jeff later apologized and said that he was nervous and had just lost it. I would have had the same reaction if I were him. What I remember most about Jeff was when he sang the song, "You've Got a Friend." He sang beautifully the song that meant so much to us as refugees. All six of us had no family in the country. All we had was one another.

Mark S. Painter was a friend with whom I felt very close. I was always comfortable hanging around with Mark, and I have many fond memories of spending time with him. Mark was a law student, and I met him when he was in his last year of school at University of Pennsylvania. He came to our apartment as often as he was able. He took us to see a movie, *Superman II*. It was the first movie I'd seen in an American theatre. For some reason, *Superman II* made me even prouder to live in America. I wanted to be an American; I wanted to save the world. I felt that Mark could see in my eyes how appreciative I was of his kindness. Mark took me downtown before the Thanksgiving holiday. I was shivering in the cold weather, so he bought me a nice green jacket—the first brand new jacket I had ever owned. Since I'd arrived in the United States, all the clothes I had were from church donations and from friends. I could not thank Mark enough for his generosity.

In late October, Mark took us to attend his wedding rehearsal, where we met his future wife, who was studying for a church ministry. She and Mark were married the next day. It was the first American wedding I attended. The ceremony was so different and quick. We Cambodians celebrate a wedding for a couple days, participating in many different ceremonies throughout the celebration. Each ceremony means something to the parents, the family, the ancestors, the bride, and the groom. We serve gourmet food to guests and family. Mark's wedding lasted less than an hour. We had wedding cake and juice. I don't remember if Mark's family had a dinner celebration that evening. We went home after the cake.

We did not see Mark as often after his marriage. We missed him. The last time I heard from him, he had passed his bar and was practicing law in Pennsylvania. He had also adopted two boys, one Vietnamese and one Cambodian.

# —— CHAPTER 30 ——

# Circle of Friends

I was told that Mr. Srey Doeun, a Cambodian Navy general, was also living in Philadelphia. Mr. Srey was a cousin of my brother-in-law. I had almost joined the navy under his command when I was in Cambodia. My parents had convinced me to attend school instead of going to war.

I was lonely living in America without a family. I thought that meeting people from my hometown would make me feel close to home. Most Cambodians living in the United States in the early 1980s bonded quickly and supported each other when they found someone who had come from their hometown. So I was excited to hear the news of Mr. Srey. I searched for his contact information and finally found him. He came to visit me twice.

Mr. Srey told me that America had turned his life upside down. His wife had left him. He lived alone in downtown Philadelphia and did not want any visitors. He enjoyed being solitary, with booze as his only companion. I felt sorry for him; he had been a powerful man in Cambodia.

Mr. Srey told me that another of my brother-in-law's cousins—Srey Leng—lived nearby. I was surprised to hear that Brother Leng was there. I told Mr. Srey that, when I'd left Cambodia, Brother Leng had still been in Kien Svay, our hometown. Mr. Srey told me that the man living in Philadelphia had assumed his younger brother's name. His real name was Srey Lom. Mr. Srey did not have contact information for Brother Lom. I remembered Brother Lom vaguely from when I was in Cambodia. Brother Lom had joined the navy with Mr. Srey after high school. Mr. Srey was with him when the Khmer Rouge took control of the country. They had come to America in 1975. Brother Lom was about four or five years older than me and much younger than Mr. Srey. I thought that I would have a better relationship with Brother Lom than with Mr. Srey, given our ages.

I went to the Cambodian association to look for Brother Lom's contact information and found him in Upper Darby, a Philadelphia suburb. I called him and hoped that he could shed some light in regard to employment and school.

"Brother Lom, this is Brother Loeun," I said into the phone. Brother Loeun was a younger brother of my brother-in-law. He was in the same school grade as I was. I thought I could joke with Brother Lom by saying that I was his first cousin.

"Brother Loeun? You are my cousin?" he replied skeptically.

I quickly responded. "No, I am sorry. I am just kidding. This is Moeurn, a brother of Savaing, your first cousin's wife. I am just happy to talk to you and thought I would get your attention when I told you that I was Loeun. I would like to see you, if possible."

"I am glad that you are here, Brother Moeun. I will see you after work today. We have a lot of things to talk about," he said.

I was so happy that he would come to see me. I sat by the window, looking out to the street, trying to spot Brother's Lom car. Later in the afternoon, a sports car pulled up to the curb in front of our apartment building. I ran downstairs to greet him. A man in a work uniform exited the car. He was rather smaller in build. I had always thought he was bigger than me, but I guessed that when we were in Cambodia, he had been a grown man while I was still a young boy.

I invited him in to our apartment and pulled out a chair for him to sit on, while I sat on the floor. I told him how lucky I was to find someone I knew from home. I couldn't keep my mouth closed. I had been smiling all day. I told him that I met his brother, Leng, and sister, Malay, in Cambodia. They had survived the Khmer Rouge. Brother Lom said that he knew it. He had an uncle whose family had come here as refugees as well. His uncle, Mr. Lap, lived within walking distant of our apartment.

"I am doing very well here," Brother Lom told me. "I live in a condo in Upper Darby. Here is my address and home phone number. Call me when you need help."

Comparing Mr. Srey and Brother Lom, was like comparing earth and heaven. Mr. Srey was doing poorly while Brother Lom claimed that he was well off in America.

After giving me his information, Brother Lom continued, "I am glad that you are here. If there is anything at all that I can do for you, let me know." Brother Lom told me that he lived alone in the condo. He played guitar in a Cambodian band. He boasted that he had lots of money. I believed him and respected him. I told brother Lom that I had just arrived here from Cleveland, and I was between school and employment. I told him that if I could get a good job, I would go to school part-time. If I did not, I would like to be a full-time student. Brother Lom told me that he would support whatever decision I made. "I have a lot of money. I can help," he assured me. I felt Brother Lom's warmth, a feeling that I had not felt since I'd left Cambodia.

I was fortunate to meet and be friends with a Cambodian dentist, Dr. Tong Hor. He had a private practice in Upper Darby, not too far from his home. Dr. Tong Hor liked to play ping-pong, and since I was a good ping-pong player, he often invited me for dinner at his home. We usually played ping-pong in the basement before and after dinner.

Dr. Tong Hor felt that my English was good enough to attend vocational school. He referred me to the Lyons Institute with a kind letter of recommendation. I took a competency exam, and I was qualified to attend the dental laboratory training. The school assisted me in applying for a vocational grant for tuition. I was still responsible for the material fees, which was about $250. I gathered all the money I had and was able to come up with $150. None of my roommates could help, since all of them were on refugee financial assistance. I thought that I could ask Brother Lom for help. I took a subway to Upper Darby to see him on the weekend. I phoned and told him that I was on the way and would like to speak with him.

After he finished with his guitar practice, Brother Lom took off the headphones. He explained, "I have to be mindful of my neighbors. When I practice, I put my headphone set on. Only I can hear. It does not bother them." Then he put down the guitar.

I had a hard time finding words to begin. I did not know what he would think but hoped that he would be excited to hear that I had been accepted to a vocational school.

"Brother Lom, Dr. Tong Hor referred me to dental lab school. I took a placement exam, and I passed it. I am so excited about this opportunity." I had goose bumps just talking about it. I continued, "I will be trained for a year to make false teeth. Dr. Tong Hor will help me find a job after I finish school." I still couldn't wipe the smile from my face.

Brother Lom looked at me with mixed emotions. "You just got a job," he pointed out. "How do you plan to handle a job and going to school?"

He was correct. I had started working at a Marriott Hotel restaurant as a dishwasher a couple of weeks earlier. I knew that I would have to juggle the job and school. I already had a plan. "Yes, brother, I already planned my schedule out. My school starts early in the morning, and it is only three and half hours a day. I'll have plenty of time to get to work. My school day ends at one o'clock and my job starts at three."

"Sounds like you know what you are doing, brother," Brother Lom said. "Is there anything I can do for you?"

I was happy to hear him ask, but I still felt shy about what I was about to say. "I am short a hundred dollars for the registration fee," I told him. "I would like to borrow this amount, and I would pay you back when I save enough money from my employment."

"If you don't have the money to pay, you shouldn't go to school," he responded, his face and voice stone cold.

I was hurt and embarrassed. I did not want to beg him either. I changed the subject of conversation and left.

When I got back, Mark was in my apartment. He wrote me a check for a hundred dollars and told me that it was a gift. "And good luck in school," he added.

Thank you, Mark!

# CHAPTER 31

# Seeking Higher Education

In my heart, I had always wanted to become a physician. I knew I could do it. I hoped that with my dental lab education and experience would get me into medical school some day. This was how little I knew about education.

One day, on my day off, I went to the Philadelphia Community College to speak with the school counselor. I wanted to register for the 1982–83 school year. I thought that by the time the term began in the fall, I would be close to finishing my vocational school. I told the school counselor that I wanted to be a physician and that I was currently enrolled in a three-month dental lab training.

He laughed. "That is not the same, son. You need a lot of preparation to attend medical school to become a physician. Your dental laboratory training does not prepare you for medical school. The college tuition is expensive. But if you have a high school diploma, we could help you apply for a Pell Grant to pay for school."

"Yes, I have high school diploma from my country. I do not have a certificate to prove it because the Khmer Rouge destroyed all such documentation."

The counselor paused. "I do not know if we would accept your country's high school diploma. However, you could get a GED here, and we could use that for the Pell Grant application."

"GED?" I asked. "What is that?"

"A GED is a high school equivalency diploma," he explained. "You could take the GED exam with the school district. You might start out by going to adult school. The Philadelphia Public Library also has a class to help you prepare for the GED exam."

I determined that I would go all the way; I would break down any barriers that might get in my way. I planned to go to the public library to register for the GED preparation class on the weekend. I arranged my schedule to continue with school and work while attending the GED class. The schedule was tight. Riding the bus and subway would not get me where I needed to be on time. I had already saved up $500. I thought I could buy a used car for transportation. The used car dealer told me that he had a $500 car, but it needed a lot of work. He said that if I had a cosigner, I could get a better, more reliable car. He pointed to a 1979 Cutlass Supreme. It was a beauty. He took me for a ride and said that the car was on sale for $2,500.

I quickly thought of Brother Lom. *He has a stable job and money in the bank. He could cosign for me*, I said to myself. I thought that he would be okay with cosigning, since it did not involve his pocket money. I was wrong.

"You are still very new to this country. You have a job, you go to school, and now you want a car," he scolded. "Having a car is a lot of responsibility. It will be much easier for you to continue riding buses and the subway."

Who was he to tell me what was easier for me? I was upset. He was right that owning a car was going to be a lot of responsibility. But hadn't he seen me display how responsible I was? I began to feel that Brother Lom was only paying me lip service. He was a barrier, not a supporter. He had not done anything to help me, as he had said he would when we first met. I needed a car so that I could get to work and school. I did not want to hear him preach about what I should do. I told myself that Brother Lom had turned me down twice; I did not want to wait for him to strike at my heart a third time. So I completely terminated my relationship with him and focused on my next step.

I managed my time so that I could go to the public library in late March 1982 to enroll for the GED preparation class. I took a placement test on the first day.

When I returned the next day for the results, the librarian took me to her office. "You did very well on the test," she told me. "I do not think you need the preparation class. I will help you put in an application for a GED test." She helped me with the application, and I was scheduled to take the exam in early May 1982.

After the examination, I thought that I had done okay with most of the exam subjects but extremely well in math. While waiting for the results, a friend from California asked me to move in with him. He told me that he was in college and that he could get me in very easily.

On the day before I moved to California, Jon Howell, my former supervisor in Phanatnikhom, Chonburi, where I had worked in the refugee camp, brought over a letter with my GED results from Philadelphia Unified School District. Jon lived in Philadelphia now, three or four blocks from my apartment. His mission in Thailand was over and he had wanted to return home to take care of his elderly mother. He had found me in January 1982. Jon had two cars, a BMW and a Volvo. He said that one of them belonged to his mother, but since she couldn't drive, he had both of them. Jon had become one of my supporters.

I was afraid to open the envelope. I handed it back to Jon. "Please open it and tell me how I did?" I asked.

Jon carefully opened the envelope. "You passed!" he exclaimed.

"What? I passed?" I exploded with excitement.

"You passed, Sam. You should consider staying in Philly. You have a lot of friends here. I wish I had found you earlier," Jon said. Jon told me that he had seen my potential to do well in America even back when we were in the refugee camp. He said that he had tried to convey this message to me on a few occasions, but he didn't think I had understood him, and he was right.

After my sour relationship with Brother Lom, I did not feel like staying around. In addition, I had a friend who told me that education in California was free. I politely declined Jon's suggestion. We took our last picture together in front of the hotel before he drove me back home.

I dropped out of my dental lab program to go to California and pursue higher education. Sina, my roommate, was upset that I was leaving Philadelphia. He felt that I was abandoning him to go to California. I didn't blame him. I would probably have felt the same, with all the work he had done to get me to Philadelphia.

I arrived in Bell Garden, California, on May 29, 1982. It was exactly a year and a day since I had come to America. My friend, Saravuth, who lived in Rosemead, helped me enroll in ESL classes for the summer at East Los Angeles College. At the time, public transportation was very poor. I rode the bus to school, but I could not do so coming back home. I had to walk, since the bus on my route didn't run after 6:00 p.m. It was about a six-mile walk, which wasn't too bad.

A week later, my neighbor told me that the bus on Atlantic ran after 6:00 p.m. Instead of a six-mile walk, I walked a mile to Atlantic Street, took a bus to Florence Avenue, and got off in the city of Bell. Then I walked about two more miles to my home. I routinely did this for the whole summer.

At the same time, I worked as a teacher's assistant for the Montebello Unified School District at Bell Garden Elementary School, from 8:00 a.m. to 11:30 a.m. By the end of the summer, I was able to pay six hundred dollars for a used 1976 Honda Civic from Horn's Auto. With my own transportation, I was able to enroll full-time in college. I took four major classes and got straight As. I was very proud of my achievement, especially when I saw my name on the honor roll list of the school newspaper and, later, received a letter of congratulations from the state senator, Joseph Montoya.

# CHAPTER 32

# How I Met My Wife

I volunteered to work as a folk dance teacher for the Cambodian Preservation Arts group of Long Beach in 1983. That was when I met Bonavy, my wife. She was a female dance instructor and a star dancer for her group. We were friends until around July of 1985, when I first asked her out. I was glad that she accepted my invitation to see a movie, *Back to the Future*, starring Michael J. Fox, and have dinner in Westminster. We saw each other every weekend after that first date. I felt that we had a good connection. When I talked, she listened with a smile. She often helped me decide what my daily plan would be. She provided me with comfort when I was sad. One time, when I was devastated after an emotional breakdown, she was there for me.

When I received news from Cambodia that my mother had passed, Bonavy was my anchor. Besides of mail, we did not have any communication with Cambodia in 1985, and so I kept in contact with my mother and family in Cambodia only through letters. I would mail my letters to a friend of mine in Paris, and she would forward them to Cambodia. By the time I received a response from my family, it would be two to three months later (Cambodia's mail system was very slow then). When I heard of my mother's passing, I felt alone. I lay on my bed face down, crying helplessly. Bonavy cried with me and assured me that I would be all right. She said that my mother would be proud of me.

As my mother used to say, "You may search for your mate all over the world and possibly all your life, but in fact, she is right under your nose." I felt that Bonavy was the one. We had known each other for two years. I had never said anything to hint to her that I was interested in making her my companion for life. I felt that it was time for me to settle down. So, on August 3, 1985, I asked for a date with a plan to propose marriage. We went to Disneyland and left after having dinner. Instead of taking my usual route, on the 22 freeway, I took local streets home. I felt that I needed more time to gather my thoughts before I proposed. I kept driving. We were almost home, and I still hadn't summoned the courage to ask. I was afraid she would reject me. If she said no, what would I do? I liked our current relationship status, and a "no" would mean an end to everything. But after reviewing all the reasons that I could come up with not to propose, my heart kept bringing me back to the fact that proposing to her now was the right time.

"Bonavy?" I asked.

"Yes," she responded.

"Oh, nothing. Sorry." I was scared to ask.

"Do you want to say something?" she asked.

"Yeah, but I don't know if I should say it."

"Go ahead. We are friends. You know me," she prompted.

*Ah ha, that's what I was afraid of; we are friends!* I looked at her nervously. "Bonavy, will you marry me?"

"Yes," she responded, as if she already knew what I was going to ask her. I felt like a big mountain had been taken off my chest and as though I were floating on air.

"Thank you, thank you!" I exclaimed excitedly.

Following my words was the longest silence of the evening. We arrived at Bonavy's house before I could think of anything to say. She had agreed to marry me. My head was full of thoughts of the future, thoughts of the past, and, of course, my love for the woman sitting next to me. I was left speechless.

I finally said the only thing I could think of as she opened the car door. "Is it okay if I pick you up tomorrow for breakfast?" I asked.

"Sure!" she responded. "We have a lot to talk about."

That was one of the happiest evenings I have ever had. I went home to tell my good friend and roommate, Tivea Tim, about the good news. He was very happy for me. At that time, we lived with Brother Alexander Keo and his wife, Hang Leng. (Keo is a common last name. Brother Alexander and I are not related.)

I woke up early to pick up Bonavy. After breakfast, we went to the park to talk. I told Bonavy that I had come to this country alone; I had no relatives, but I had many friends. "And after we are married,

I will no longer have to visit friends to be offered Cambodian food," I gushed.

She smiled and then broke out into laughter.

"Do you think I cook?" she asked.

I nodded my head.

"No, I don't cook," she said very clearly.

*As a Cambodian girl, she must know how to cook. She is just being modest*, I thought.

She continued. "Marriage takes a lot of planning and money," Bonavy pointed out. "What is your plan and how much money do you have for the marriage?"

That was a fair question. Frankly, I didn't have any money at that time. I thought that we could get married next summer, after I had saved up enough money.

"At this minute, Bonavy, I don't have any money saved," I confided. "I thought that I could ask Bong Alexander and his wife to arrange for the engagement ceremony with your mother. It does not cost much for the engagement. We could do this before school starts in the fall. What do you think?" I asked her.

Bonavy agreed with my plan. But she thought that I was being modest when I said that I had no money. No Cambodian man would ask a girl to marry him when he had no savings. We would laugh at this later. When Bonavy said she did not know how to cook, she literally meant it, and I was being honest about the money. *I didn't have any!*

August 1985, engagement ceremony

From far right, Alexander, Gloria, Sorya, Samoeurn, Hang Leng, and friends

August 1985, Samoeurn and Bonavy's engagement
ring exchange ceremony

\*   \*   \*

The engagement ceremony went well. Everyone exploded with laughter before the ring ceremony because the elder family member of the bride-to-be claimed that not many people on the bride's side knew me. They had many questions about me, especially my physical appearance. The elder asked me to stand up in the middle of about thirty-five people who sat on the mat. I did, and he asked me to turn around. I did as I was told. When I sat back down, they all laughed again, and the elder said that he was just teasing me and had not thought that I would spin around for him.

We planned to get married the following year. The wedding was set for June 28, 1986. Bonavy and I worked as a team to plan our wedding. We went to the print shop to design our wedding invitation. We decided the traditional ceremony would be at Alexander's home. Traditionally, the wedding ceremony is at the bride's home, but since Alexander's home was bigger, we agreed to have it there. We never heard any comment from Bonavy's mother. Whenever we asked her for an opinion, she said it was up to us to plan the wedding.

We also planned to have a dinner reception at the Pailin Restaurant in Long Beach. To reserve the restaurant, we needed to put down a deposit. I was low on cash, so Bonavy and I agreed to take out a bank loan, which we hoped to pay back right after the wedding. The guests at a Cambodian wedding reception dinner offer gifts of money. Usually, the gifts are enough to cover all the expenses, and sometimes there is enough left over for a honeymoon. We were confident this plan would work out for us.

We both begin to distribute the wedding invitations to family and guests in April and May.

Samoeurn and Bonavy's wedding invitation
June 28, 1986

Bonavy's mother found out about the bank loan for the wedding and was very upset. She felt that, if I did not have the money for a wedding, I should never have asked her daughter to marry me. She forbade Bonavy from seeing me. She warned that, if we went through the wedding as planned, she would embarrass us during the ceremony. I was devastated. Bonavy and I tried to explain the situation, but her mother refused to hear it. My mother-in-law-to-be broke our engagement; she broke my heart and her daughter's as well. I was embarrassed in my community, especially with my many friends who had come to my engagement ceremony. (More than fifty of them had been in attendance.)

I relocated to Rosemead as soon as I could, where I lived with my friend Saravuth. I needed to be away from Long Beach and Bonavy's family.

Three days after I had arrived in Rosemead, Bonavy showed up at my home.

"I tried to reason with her," Bonavy sobbed. "My mother is hotheaded. She won't listen."

Still crying, she told me that her mother had forbidden her from mentioning my name around the house. "I have had enough of her," she concluded. Bonavy was fed up with her mother; she believed it was her life and not her mother's. She did not want to go back home.

I begged Bonavy to return home. I did not want people to think that I had broken up her family.

"Bonavy, it is my karma," I explained. "Since I left Cambodia, many of my girlfriends' mothers have not liked me because I am an orphan. They want to know the family background of the person who will marry their daughter. They want to make sure, through my family history, that I am a dependable person. All they knew about me is what they have heard from me. It is hard for them to trust, and I don't blame them. I believe that, when my time comes, I will be wed."

"But I am here, Sam. I am yours," Bonavy replied. "We will have a good life together. I don't care what others think or say of us. The matter is only between you and me."

Bonavy was right, but I was still uncomfortable that we did not have a blessing from the elders in her family. We cancelled our wedding reception. I phoned all my friends who had already received the notice and told them of the wedding cancellation. When I spoke to them, I gave no reason but said my wedding was merely postponed.

Bonavy and I went to Las Vegas on Memorial Day and got married.

May 31, 1986, Bonavy and Samoeurn
Las Vegas, Nevada

\*　　\*　　\*

Some years later, in 1995 or '96, Bonavy and I went to speak with Bonavy's mother. Douglas, our first son, was about eight months old. Bonavy was set against having anything to do with her mother, but I felt strongly that she needed to see her grandson. My mother-in-law was very pleased when she held her grandson for the first time. Douglas, our small son, helped reconcile Bonavy's relationship with her mother and brought us back together as a family.

# CHAPTER 33

# Continuing My Education

During my second semester at East Los Angeles College, my car started to give me a lot of problems. I kept missing classes because my car wouldn't start, and at one point, it stalled in the middle of the freeway. I was in need of a better car. I had no savings or credit to buy a car. My school grades began to plummet due to my absences and inability to keep up with the class work. I dropped half of my classes to stabilize my grades.

I told a friend, Lim Sok Chea, an instructional assistant for Santa Ana Unified School District (SAUSD), about my problems. Mr. Chea said that he could help me get a full-time job with SAUSD; the extra work would enable me to save enough money to buy a better car. With Mr. Chea's help, I was able to get a full-time job at the district. The problem was that I could no longer attend school full-time. I registered part-time with Rancho Santiago College in 1985.

I was later promoted to special instructional assistant. My job was to teach math to resource special program (RSP) students in middle school. These sixth to eighth graders who came to my class were far behind where they should be. Some of them still had difficulty with basic arithmetic. I had six to ten students per period and six periods per day. I stayed after school for two hours, and I encouraged the students to come in for extra help. Most of the students who came after school for extra help entered algebra class the next school year. I was proud of my work and felt that I could do this for the rest of my life. So I changed my studies and focused on math.

I successfully completed my associate's of sciences in mathematics degree in 1987 and enrolled in a four-year college. Due to multiple circumstances—including my difficulties with English and my ability to obtain a single-subject credential in mathematics, I ended up graduating with a bachelor's in business administration (BBA) in 1989.

After graduation, I left SAUSD to get a job with the county government as an eligibility technician. I came to realize that pursuing my dream of becoming a physician, given my current situation, was almost impossible. However, I still wanted to pursue a higher education. I immediately enrolled in a master's program.

I received a master's degree in human behavior in 1991. My wife and I had a small party to celebrate this milestone. I was happy and laughed until I felt that my shoulders couldn't take any more shaking.

\*    \*    \*

"Honey, wake up. We are home." My wife shook my shoulder gently.

I brushed my eyes with my forearm and pulled myself up. We had arrived in Los Angeles on the same day we left. I felt exhausted from traveling and from the emotional roller coaster I had been on since leaving Cambodia.

June 1999, graduation ceremony at United States International University, (from left) Douglas, Samoeurn, Beauregard, Bonavy, and Nickolas

# CHAPTER 34

# New Work Assignment

During my first year of employment with Orange County, I was fortunate to forge a friendship with Princess Santa Sisowath Smith, a daughter of the former Cambodian vice president. The princess worked for the Department of Mental Health in the same county. She felt that, with my refugee experience and education, I could be a great asset to the Cambodian community if I were to join the mental health workforce. Without any reservation, I applied for the position.

With the princess's referral, Mr. Ken White, a county service chief, hired me as case manager/mental health specialist with Orange County in November 1991. I was later transferred to work under the supervision of Mr. Bill Murray. I felt that this position fit me like a glove. As case manager, my job was to help our mental health consumers meet their basic needs, such as food and shelter. I was also responsible for case management—helping mental health consumers put their life back together after incarceration, hospitalization, or a mental health breakdown. I occasionally performed crisis intervention, putting clients who were a danger to themselves or others or who were gravely disabled on seventy-two-hour holds. I enjoyed helping others restore their daily living activities. I helped clients meet basic needs by finding, for example, a nice board-and-care home for them to live in. I felt that it was a privilege to serve them, since I had been in a situation much like theirs and had not received that kind of help. I did very little counseling. I referred those who needed therapy to the clinical unit for counseling. Ms. Smith was in the clinical unit, under the supervision of Ms. Mai Cong. We were a good team and worked together to help our clients.

I had a long-standing history of working in the helping profession. In the refugee camps, I had volunteered to work in a tuberculosis ward, with the Catholic Relief Services (CRS), and for Save the Children. I was a longtime member of the Cambodian Preservation Arts group of Long Beach. I helped educate children about gangs and drugs in the community. I was a former member of the board of directors of the United Cambodian Community (UCC) and the Cambodian Advisory Council (CAC). I wanted to advance my career and wanted to serve in a higher role in a mental health setting. So in 1993, I enrolled in a doctoral program for clinical psychology at the United States International University. I felt that with the new set of skills I would gain, I would be better able to serve people in need.

Up until June 1993, I served a mixed population, doing case management. Then the county adopted "the rehabilitation model." This model called for collapsing the two separate units—the case management and the clinical unit—into one. Now, instead of doing only case management, I was also responsible for conducting mental health interventions. I was transferred to work with Ms. Mai Cong in Ms. Smith's unit. In this unit, I was assigned to work solely with Cambodian clients. This population was primarily experiencing post-traumatic stress disorder (PTSD) and major depressive disorder, a severe mental health issue. I was not mentally prepared for this assignment, but I was glad that I had been given the opportunity to work with my people. I read as many books as I could get my hands on, hoping that I would be able to serve my clients well.

Unfortunately, after listening to multiple stories from consumers who reported that they were tortured and left for dead, I began to be affected by their tales.

# CHAPTER 35

# Traumatized Again

Most of my clients suffered from either PTSD or major depressive symptoms. I listened daily to their problems and tried to help them cope with their difficulties. I tried very hard to keep my past trauma aside while working with the clients.

Before I knew it, I started to experience "countertransference." Countertransference can be both negative and positive, depending on how the individual reacts to the situation. For me, I reacted negatively. I allowed myself to be vulnerable to the situation. My symptoms began with guilt, nightmares, and flashbacks about my brother's death. I felt guilty for not being able to help my family. I believed I was to blame for my brother's death, and that guilt weighed heavily on me. I could hear every single word my mother had said to me the morning that my baby brother had died, almost as if she were in the room. The vision of his body and the sound of my mother's voice felt very real, as if it were happening all over again, and I saw the body and heard her words simultaneously. I had never given myself a chance to speak to my mother about my brother's death. She had passed away in 1985 of ovarian cancer. I was not able to attend her funeral because, at that time, Cambodia was still closed to the outside world.

A few months earlier, I had returned to Cambodia to look for my father's grave. I asked the old people who still lived in the village if they knew where he had been buried. No one knew. I felt terrible for not being able to find his grave to pay my respects. I could not even find the burial ground of my brother, who I had buried. I blamed myself for the losses of my family members.

I remember reading a Socrates quote in an Alfred Adler book. "The life unexamined is the life not worth living." I began to examine my life. I found that I had made many mistakes, most of which I had not forgiven myself for. I was the one who had insisted that we go west for a better life, but it turned out that many of our family members had died. Everyone in my uncle's family who stayed in Chroy Ampil had survived the holocaust. If I had listened to my father and withdrawn our name from leaving Temple Champa as my cousin had suggested, everyone would still be alive, like my uncle's family. I felt responsible for the deaths in my family. I felt that my life was not worth living. The depression and stress overwhelmed me.

I began to have nightmares, then recurring nightmares. I was afraid to go to bed. Every time I closed my eyes, I saw myself being dragged and repeatedly beaten. I had never had the courage to fight back against the Khmer Rouge; even in the dream I did not fight back. Sometimes, I saw my mother blame me for not giving rice to my baby brother. In the dream, I attempted to ask my mother for forgiveness, but my jaw seemed locked.

I kept telling myself, *This was just a dream; it is just a dream. You could fight back against the Khmer Rouge; you could talk to your mother. It would help restore your confidence, and it might help your current sleep difficulty.*

I determined to get better sleep. I told myself that I must fight back if I were to be dragged out again. I slowly confronted my torturers in the dream, and finally, I physically fought back. Sometimes, our fights were intense. On the second night of fighting back, I heard my wife screaming. I jumped out of bed. I found myself soaked with sweat.

My wife put her hands on her face. "You hit me in the face!" she told me. "What is wrong with you?"

"I am sorry," I told her. "I had a dream. I saw myself fighting with the Khmer Rouge. I must have moved my hand toward you when I attempted to punch the Khmer Rouge guard."

My wife had bruises on her face the next morning. Now, she joined my sleeplessness. She was afraid of getting hit again in her sleep. I was afraid to fall asleep. I did not want to see the Khmer Rouge pull me out in my dream, and I could not defend myself because I was afraid of accidentally hitting my wife again. We found a solution that would allow at least one of us to sleep. I am a lefty. In the dream, I never punched the Khmer Rouge across my body. So if we switched sides of the bed, my wife should be safer. She moved to my right side. After that, she never got hit again.

I continued to have nightmares. My nightmares expanded from the recurring dream to include anything that scared me, and I struggled to stay awake. Staying awake when I was so drowsy was difficult. I kept hearing my mother's voice: *If you just gave your brother some of your rice, he would still be alive.*

The voices did not bother me as much as the guilt—the guilt that I felt over not doing what she had asked was eating me alive.

Because of lack of sleep and hardly eating, I was easily irritated and angry. I had difficulty focusing, and I was easily startled. My mind wandered off while I was in session with my clients. I knew that I was no longer able to function normally in my position as therapist. I realized that my PTSD symptoms interfered greatly with my ability to provide fair services to my client.

In the midst of this emotional roller coaster, I asked my supervisor to leave early. I hopped in my 1986 Toyota Celica and drove off. I do not remember the streets or the freeway I was on when I left work. I found myself at the Rim of the World High School in San Bernardino Mountains. It was late in the afternoon. I walked to the edge of the cliff, contemplating suicide.

I went back to the car and steered my wheels toward the cliff, with the intention of driving off. "I can't take it anymore," I screamed at the top of my lungs. "I am worthless. Why didn't I or couldn't I do something to protect my family? I am a coward. They depended on me. Why am I so selfish?"

My head ached, and it felt like it was going to explode. I argued with myself. "If you die now, who is going to take care of your brothers and sisters in Cambodia? You saw them twice in the last ten years. You know how needy they were. Is this how you want them to remember you?"

I backed the car up and drove back home. My wife was very concerned. I decided to keep what had happened to myself and didn't tell her where I had been.

# CHAPTER 36

# The Treatment of PTSD

It had been a week since my recurring nightmares had been accompanied with intense suicidal thoughts. Ms. Smith noticed the change and asked me to her office.

"You don't look like yourself. What is going on?" she asked.

"I think I have PTSD, Bong" I replied. I trusted Ms. Smith, so I told her what I had been experiencing for the last week. I told her about my trip to the mountain the previous day.

She told me that I'd had a serious PTSD breakdown. She suggested that I see someone for help. "You cannot see your clients when you are in this condition," she added.

She told me that she could make an arrangement for me to see Dr. William Young. "He will be able to treat you or refer you to someone who can help."

Dr. Young was a clinical psychologist who worked part-time for Orange County. He had a full-time private practice, and he practiced psychoanalysis. I always liked and respected Dr. Young. He was also respected by his clients. He always dressed in suits and seemed very calm. I agreed to see him.

"Santa told me you have trouble sleeping. Can you tell me about it?" Dr. Young asked.

"I do not know if I have a problem with sleeping. I am afraid to fall asleep. Every time I close my eyes, I have nightmares. These are recurring nightmares—the same theme, over and over."

"Can you tell me what those nightmares are about?"

I told Dr. Young about my intrusive dreams. I recalled the time I had been beaten because of the cigarette lighter and the constant threats to my life during the Khmer Rouge regime. I told him that the previous night, I'd had a different dream—one that I clearly remembered. I saw myself in the water at a stream. I tried to cross to the other side, but there was a large fallen tree in the middle of the stream. When I climbed on the tree, I saw snakes. There were snakes everywhere. I froze. I screamed for help, but I had no voice. As usual, I jumped out of the bed, soaking with sweat.

After listening to my story and my dreams, Dr. Young told me that I had made many decisions in the past that I was not proud of. The dreams and nightmares were from my subconscious. He used the here and now to help me get in touch with reality. "You are here now," Dr. Young told me. "You are safe. There is no Khmer Rouge around. You have a family who supports you."

He suggested that I explore what had helped me cope with the problems in the past. "You need to search for appropriate coping skills, if you do not yet have them," he explained.

Dr. Young also suggested that I see a therapist on an ongoing basis until the problems subsided. He said that he could not see me because of the clinic relationship. I did not follow through with his recommendation because of trust issues. I was paranoid. I did not trust anyone.

I was tired of being fearful of my nightmares and easily startled. I kept thinking about killing myself to end all of this. Fortunately, I had enough courage to tell my wife, my coworkers, and my supervisor about my suicidal thoughts and my stressful feelings. They said that they were surprised that I had been doing so well despite what I had gone through in the killing fields. They actually were not surprised that I had PTSD symptoms.

Mai Cong, my supervisor, referred me to the Employees Assistance Program (EAP) in Orange County. She also encouraged me to take as much time off as I needed to get myself better. I went to the EAP that afternoon and met with a therapist named Veronica Kelley. I remember her name because it sounded like she had two first names. After I had briefly told her about my difficulties, she told me that I should be able to handle it. "You are a very strong person," she said. "You enrolled in a doctoral program. You are a smart man."

I knew that Ms. Kelley was trying to empower me with self-confidence and self-determination. Her intentions were good. But I did not feel that Ms. Kelley understood me. To be fair, I did not tell Ms. Kelley everything I had experienced. Trusting people I did not know was still a problem. I went home feeling hopeless.

The next morning, I went to see Dr. Nhu Tran, a staff psychiatrist who I worked with. Dr. Tran was a gentleman. He carefully listened to my problems. He made me feel like I was the one person that he was most concerned about and that he wanted to help me. He assured my safety. He gave me a sample bag of Prozac and suggested that I take 20 mg a day, adding that I could take as much as 60 mg a day. He asked me to stop by his office five or ten minutes a day so that he could monitor my progress.

I was still depressed and stressed after a week went by. Dr. Tran told me that it would take three to four weeks before the medication kicked in, but I felt that I did not have that much time to live. *Patience* was the last word I wanted to hear. I wanted my problem fixed now! As a new therapist, I knew that emotional problems did not get fixed in one day. But as a consumer, I wanted to get well now. If I had a headache, I would take a Tylenol or Advil and expect the headache to go away in three to four hours. I couldn't wait for three to four weeks to get better. That was impossible.

I made an appointment to see a therapist at Kaiser Permanente in Anaheim. I was scheduled to see a licensed clinical social worker. I was angry when he told me that I was strong and I should be able to handle my problems, since I had been smart enough to enroll in a doctoral problem. He sounded like Ms. Kelley. I felt hopeless. I left Kaiser and drove up the mountain.

*This time for sure, I am going to kill myself. I am done. No one can help me. I am helpless*, I thought. I sped all the way up the mountain without concern for my safety or that of others. I stopped at the outlook, over 6,000 feet in elevation. I got out of the car, still angry with myself.

But I couldn't help but feel the November mountain breeze on my face. I took a deep breath, walked toward a gigantic rock, and sat down. The clean air of the mountain breeze must have killed the toxins in my brain. I remembered so many playful memories with my little brothers before the war. I remembered my parents telling us to love one another and saying that, as a big brother, I should take care of them all, because I was the one who would take their place when they were gone. I remembered how much they had emphasized the importance of higher education.

Education? My mind went back to my classroom, Dr. Mason's clinical assessment class. Dr. Mason always wrote a quote on the chalkboard before he began his class. One of the quotes that I remembered was, "All babies are beautiful and every mother has one."

*Oh my God*, I realized, *my mother must have thought that I was her beautiful baby. And what do I do now? Wanting to kill myself? I have not even had a child of my own. I should have a baby.*

I needed to go home and tell my wife that we should have a baby.

Just like that, I returned home. I told my wife all about my symptoms in detail. I told her about my flashbacks, my suicidal thoughts, my nightmares, and what had made me think differently. I wanted to get better and to have a baby. As everyone I had met in the past therapy sessions had told me, I am strong. I could do it. I just needed the time to heal. Why couldn't I see it before?

My wife was very understanding. She said she would like me to focus on my well-being first and then we would work together on our next goal.

I went to see a therapist for short-term counseling. I continued to follow my medication regimen, 60 mg of Prozac a day. I took two weeks off from work to put myself back together.

During the time off, my friend, Tivea, took me and my wife fishing. We were in the boat between the port of Long Beach and Catalina Island. I did not catch any fish, while others in the boat caught plenty. We went ocean fishing a couple of times. Vannarith, my other friend, took me fishing at Skinner Lake the following week. We left home before sunrise and came back around 8:30 p.m. Vannarith gave me some of the fish he had caught. Although I did not catch any fish on any of the trips, I was happy to be on the open water with friends and fresh air. I felt like my stress dissolved in the air.

My condition began to improve further when my former supervisor, Mr. Bill Murray, asked me to join his unit, working with dual-diagnoses clients, clients who had mental health and drug issues. Very few to none of the Cambodian clients were among this population.

# CHAPTER 37

# The Road to Recovery

In the spring of 1994, I took a philosophy class called "A Social Person in Social Context." Professor Dil Anwar assigned a final paper with the topic, "Who or what is making you who you are today?" He also required us to present the paper in class.

Since I had been attending therapy sessions for my PTSD, I was able to comfortably share my feelings and my past with the therapist and very close friends. I felt that it was time for me to open up to others. I wanted the whole world to know what I had been through. I wanted them to know what happened in Cambodia between 1975 and 1979, how it affected me, and how it affected millions of Cambodians. An estimated 1.7 million died during the Cambodian holocaust. That was almost a third of the country's population.

I began my class presentation talking about when I was a child and worked my way through to the time that I was in the holocaust. I was interrupted many times with my own tears and choked up while telling my story.

The professor came and put his arm around my shoulders. "Do you want to stop now? It's okay; you can stop," he told me.

"No, I want to finish it. I have to be able to finish my story."

I kept on talking. What follows is a quote from the end of my presentation:

Many Cambodian immigrants settled in the United States and in many other countries around the world after 1979, having gone through tough times and suffering during the Khmer Rouge regime just as I had. Many of them seek emotional support from therapists. Cultural, stigma, and language barriers often play important roles in the treatment processes.

I believe God is giving me a mission to help them. My flashback experiences will help me to understand more how others are affected and how they can learn to cope with their activities and daily lives. I learned how hard it was to feel hopeless, feelings that I did not experience while living under the Khmer Rouge regime. I understand how devastating it is to experience suicidal thoughts and the intense feelings associated with those thoughts. I have learned to express my feelings to others. I agree that these dreadful experiences will stay in me and could resurface when I encounter stressful events. I understand that I need tools to prevent and deal with that when it occurs. I understand that my pain can affect my work performance if not treated. I am grateful to have my family and so many great friends for support. I am happy that I am choosing the clinical psychology field for my career. I thank God, who has been watching over me and gives me strength to survive. Now that I know my pain, the next step is to build up my strength so I can deal with it. Hopefully in the near future, I will be able to better serve my people and others who suffer similar symptoms.

I ended my presentation with a happy cry. My classmates provided me with empathetic feedback. I remember a few who pulled me aside to give me their support. My classmate Bill (I am sorry to say that I forget his last name), who was a Ventura Community College professor, was crying tears of joy that I was able to survive the holocaust. He assured me of his availability if I ever needed help. Pete Wilkerson wrote me a two-page feedback letter analyzing my journey. He pointed out the negative and positive aspects of the decision I had made during the stressful time. He stressed the strength it took me to survive and to keep my family as one. He assured me that I had done all I could do to help my family, including my desire for us to "stay together" during a time of intense pressure. He pointed out that, even if I had shared my rice with my brother, I had no way of knowing that he would still be alive. It was his time to go.

I was not surprised to hear the overwhelming support from my peers. However, I was surprised that I was able to make it through the whole presentation. This breakthrough encouraged me to keep on talking about my difficulties and to solicit coping skills from friends, who were, for the most part, in the mental health profession. What helped me the most was being able to talk with people about my problems, whether it was in a one-on-one setting or making a presentation to a large group.

Samoeurn at the California Endowment, August 23, 2011
Presentation Topic: A Cambodian Journey to Recovery

# CHAPTER 38

# Out of the Dark

No human being should ever be put through the torturous and traumatizing situations that I and so many other Cambodians had to face. I lived in constant fear for my life during that four-year period. Dr. David Kinzie of Oregon University labeled Cambodians' PTSD, "a wound that will never heal."

The treatment for a person who suffered from prolonged exposure to trauma like I did has not been around for very long, so not much help was available when I had my full-blown PTSD. It is fair to say that I was also having major depressive symptoms. I was sad every day. I had no interest in any pleasurable activities, and I lost a significant amount of weight. I felt tired all the time. I had concentration problems and recurrent thoughts of death. I was fraught with guilt over my brother's death and the inability to take care of my family during the crisis.

Treating prolonged trauma exposure mixed with major depressive symptoms is complicated. A few experts in the field of anxiety and depressive disorders among Cambodians proposed a combination of diagnoses called "complicated grief" because of the nature of what we suffered. They described complicated grief as the experience of a number of symptoms, including traumatic distress, flashbacks, feelings of futility about the future, numbness, detachment, difficulty acknowledging death, feeling that life is empty or meaningless, feeling that part of oneself has died, recurrent suicidal thoughts, guilt, loss of a sense of control, mistrust, irritability, and anger related to death.

Researchers have proven the most recent cognitive behavioral therapy (CBT), such as trauma focus and seeking safety, to be helpful for those suffering PTSD and depression. Those therapies could have helped me to cope with my trauma if they had been available when I was unstable. I was told that eye movement desensitization and reprocessing, also known as EMDR therapy, could help.

I very much wanted to get out of this darkness I found myself in. I believed that there was no such thing as a "one size fits all" treatment. I knew I must try everything to help myself to find the light of happiness.

My mental health condition was not a common PTSD as defined in the *Diagnostic and Statistical Manual of Mental Disorders* (DSM). Our traumatic experiences, such as threats to life, did not happen once or twice; rather, these threats were repeated daily for more than three years. Mental health professionals often focus more on trauma focus CBT, seeking safety, and finding coping skills for PTSD treatment. There are probably more than a hundred coping skills that you could find in PTSD treatment. I am going to tell you which of those have worked for me and the few that I worked with after I was able to control my symptoms in 1994.

Talking therapy definitely worked. The therapist began by assuring my safety, "You are here now. You are safe. The Khmer Rouge is not going to hurt you." She worked with me for a couple of sessions on recognizing the here and now until I felt secure enough to open up. After I presented her with my life story, my therapist worked with me on coping skills. A handful of coping skills worked for me, a person with complex PTSD. I was made aware of possible triggers of my flashbacks and nightmares.

The trauma and torture ended in April 1979. Why did it take fourteen years for me to experience the PTSD symptoms?

I realized that from 1979 to 1993, I was in the honeymoon period. I partied with friends and focused on school. In 1992, I visited my family for the first time since I had left them. That was after the end of my first semester in my doctoral program. During the summer of 1992, with the pressure to help my poor family back home, my school work, and my employment, I became overwhelmingly stressed. With my savings and an additional loan from the bank, I went back to Cambodia in the summer of 1993. I was happy to see them again, but I was sad that I was not able to help them enough. I went to the village to look for my brother's grave, and I couldn't find it. The nightmares began when I returned to America.

It appeared that being overwhelmed with stress *triggered* the PTSD symptoms. I learned to avoid being overwhelmed and kept my stress to a minimum. I scheduled ongoing activities, such as fishing, camping, or just going to the beach. I allowed myself to *cry* when I was sad. It released my depression and anxiety. I relearned that I must *never give up* on life. I learned to *forgive* myself and *accept* the past instead, of *blaming* myself. I recognized my limitations; I can't do everything. I had to learn to believe in myself again.

I took 60 mg of Prozac daily for about a month. I do not know if it was the placebo effect, but my mind started to clear up, and I was able to reason intelligently.

In the subsequent sessions, the therapist asked me to explore what was important to me. For me, that was easy. My family was everything to me. I wanted to be able to help my family and to make them proud of me. The question was how would I achieve that goal? This goal was not a new one. My parents had implanted it in my soul. I never thought of it that way until I explored it with a therapist who I trusted. My therapist encouraged me to develop a goal-setting plan. We set goals that were achievable, both long-term goals and short-term goals. I would reward myself with vacations or time to myself each time I reached the goal. I was praised every time I achieved my short-term goal. The praise validated my ability to control my destiny.

One of my wishes was to have a child the following year. I had medical complications that interfered with my ability to have a natural biological child. With my persistence and never-give-up attitude and the help of God, my wife was able to conceive, and we were blessed with a son, Douglas. Douglas means "the chosen one," and he is. That was a milestone that we knew we wanted to reach, but we never thought that we could get there that quickly.

As I mentioned earlier, Cambodian PTSD is a complex one. It is a wound that never heals. As is the case with a person who has recovered from drug or alcohol abuse, a person with Cambodian PTSD can experience relapse at any time. Knowing the triggers will help you to design your own relapse prevention plan. I was tortured many times when it was raining. Therefore, I become sad and depressed when it is overcast for more than a day or so. As long as I am busy and keep my mind off the weather, I am okay. So, when it is overcast and I am at home, I usually go to the movies or plan activities with my family.

I am out of the dark now. I will keep myself this way till the end of my time.

October 22, 2011, Keo family

(from left) Douglas, Beauregard, Bonavy, Samoeurn, and Nickolas
Photo by Saravuth Tauch

# Keo's Family Tree
## Paternal

Maternal

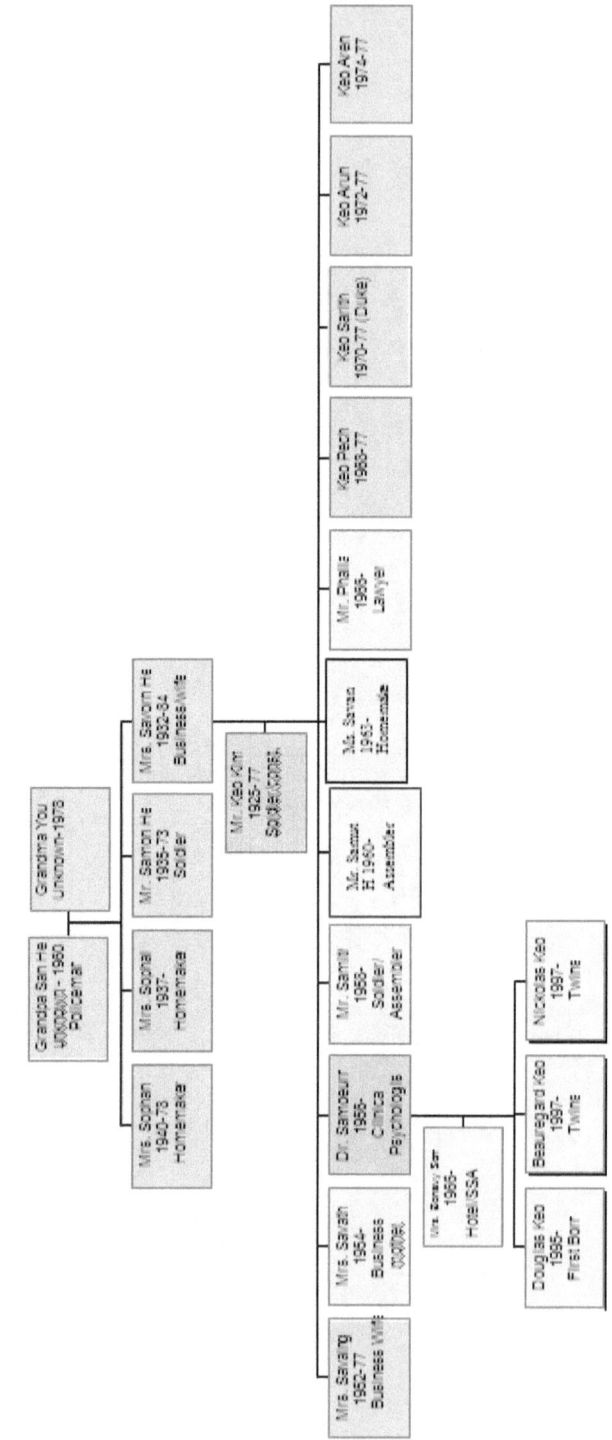

# BIOGRAPHY

Dr. Sam Keo is a licensed clinical psychologist working for the County of Los Angeles. He has also been a visiting lecturer at California State University at Long Beach. He is the third son of the eleven children of Mr. Keo Kim and Mrs. He Savoan. Although his father, Mr. Keo, only had three years of formal education and Mrs. He, his mother, had never been to school, both of them greatly valued higher education. They inspired Dr. Keo to never give up and to pursue his dreams and goals no matter what challenges or difficulties might come to be in his way.

Dr. Keo arrived in this country in 1981 as a refugee from war-torn Cambodia. Not only did he have to learn English, but he also had to learn to survive. He was greeted with a discouraging experience when, upon his arrival in the United States, a caseworker told him that he would not be anything but a slave to the Americans. He struggled to educate himself. He earned a GED and, ultimately, a doctorate in psychology. His own experience with post-traumatic stress and his journey to recovery deepened Dr. Keo's compassion for the struggles of others and his enduring commitment to helping his community.

Dr. Keo does not forget his past, nor is he ashamed of it.

Dr. Keo is conscientious and diligent in regard to his work and professional ethics. He received an award for community service from the Latino Behavioral Health Institute in 2008 for generously giving time and support toward the advancement of the Latino Behavioral Health Institute. His psychologist peers nominated him for the departmental employee of the year in 2009. He was recognized by the California Institution of Mental Health at the statewide Cultural Competence Mental Health Summit XVI and was awarded the Statewide Cultural Competence Professional Award in 2009.

He is a loving husband and a father of three sons.

# MY OWN WORDS OF WISDOM

The Lord Buddha taught us that life is like a floating particle in the stream. Sometimes it goes quickly; other times it goes slowly. At times, it goes through a rough spot, but just remember that its journey will end in the same place. I saw my particle of life go through a rough, rocky spot and flow into the constant water current. I have to be flexible if I want to survive this horrific time.

www.ingramcontent.com/pod-product-compliance
Lightning Source LLC
Chambersburg PA
CBHW061250280526
45784CB00002B/709